SWAY

Principled Influence and Ethical Persuasion

The ~~Un~~likely Connection Between Autism and Influence

JOHN HENDERSON

John Henderson
PUBLISHING
SINCE 2014

© 2018 John Henderson

All rights reserved. No portion of this book my be reproduced, stored in a retrial system, or transmitted in any form or by any means-electronic, mechanical, photocopy, recording, scanning or other- except for brief quotations in critical review or articles, without the prior written permission of the publisher.

Published by John Henderson.

John Henderson titles may be purchased in bulk for educational, business, fund-raising, or sales promotional use. For more information please e-mail requests to john@johnhenderson.org

ISBN 9781981027040

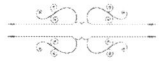

It was said in ancient Rome that when Cicero spoke people applauded, but when Demosthenes spoke, people marched!

-Jim Rohn

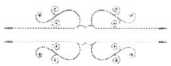

Contents

Authors Note

Introduction

Section 1: Charisma and the Art of Spreading Passion
Chapter 1   A Great Hero. . .
Chapter 2   What Good Fortune. . .

Section 2: Kindness, The Power Behind Persuasion
Chapter 3   If I Have Seen Further. . .
Chapter 4   One is Only Happy. . .

Section 3: Psychopaths and Oxytocin
Chapter 5   This Scandal. . .
Chapter 6   I Didn't Know. . .

Section 4: Humility, The Absence of Arrogance
Chapter 7   Now Moses Was. . .
Chapter 8   The Biggest Challenge. . .

Section 5: Social Interaction
Chapter 9   This is my Letter. . .
Chapter 10   People Arrive at. . .

Section 6: How the Few Influence the Many
Chapter 11   Worldly Wisdom Teaches. . .
Chapter 12   If Everyone is Thinking Alike. . .

The Beginning
Chapter 13   Progress is Impossible. . .

To Grandma and Po.
You spent my entire life serving the underprivileged, helping the forgotten and cheering for the underdogs. Thank you for a lifetime of examples.

Authors Note

You want more influence.

You may not think in those terms, but you certainly want your coworkers to listen to what you say, your employees to work in the manner in which you have trained them or your kids to understand the value in your lectures.

That last one may be tough, but this book will help you have more influence in every area of life, even with your kids.

How do I know?

I have an incredible insight into the power of influence. Like most authors on books about influence, I have experienced high stress sales environments, signed 6 figure deals, spoken to large audiences, built million dollar businesses and felt the pressure and power of influence in the moment.

But I have a perspective most of those authors don't. Because even though I can draw from those high level experiences, nothing impressed me more than an instant that occurred while I was being booked into jail.

I started out my adult life as a high school dropout, with a few addictions, living on the couches made available by my friends, the back seat of my car or wherever I happened to pass out that night.

It's a far cry from being the successful business owner, speaker and author that I find when I look in the mirror today.

But in the late 90's I was in and out of jail. On the occasion in question I had caused a major ruckus with my neighbors and was being booked into the Coconino County jail for some troubling crimes. During this process it was customary for me to scowl at the corrections officer, to show him or her just how tough I thought I was.

As I turned the corner after being fingerprinted I prepared my best tough-guy face for the guard. I shot my usual glare in the direction of where I knew the officer would be and I melted.

The officer was not a stranger. He was a young man, just a few years older than me. His name was Kenny, but I didn't have to read his badge to know that.

Kenny had gone to high school with me.

We were 200 miles from the school where I had failed to graduate, but that Kenny had proudly conquered. Our paths crossed two mountain ranges away from where we grew up. As my tough guy face faded, Kenny looked at me sadly.

He was not angry, arrogant or overly physical, which were three things I had come to expect from the Department of Corrections. He was hurt, he had empathy, but most of all, it seemed that he cared.

Kenny hadn't known me well, but in our tiny school no one went un-noticed. I'm sure, like most of us it was a shock for Kenny to see just how far down a fellow classmate could fall. Then he said two sentences that changed my life.

"What are you doing here man?"

It wasn't an accusation, it was remorseful. There was a heavy emphasis on the word 'here', as if to say, "of all the places." He was saying, you could be so much more than the guy I'm herding into this cell.

In that moment I felt something inside of me. As soon as I felt it, Kenny said exactly what I was feeling with his second and final sentence. It was the last thing I ever heard him say. I have not encountered him since, but if I do I will hug him and tell him that, on that dark night, under the cold fluorescent lights in the Coconino County jail he spoke one of the most influential sentences ever spoken to me.

He said, "You're better than this."

That moment showed me the power of empathetic and caring influence. It taught me the difference between trying to force change on someone, and showing a person they are worth making a better choice.

There are millions of words written about how to coerce prospects, buyers or clients into buying what you want. This is not one of those books. I wanted to find out how to ethically influence people into better choices, like Kenny did for me decades ago. In my study on influence I found an incredible source of kindness and compassionate influence.

I think that, like me, you will be amazed at what I learned.

Introduction

"I'm for truth, no matter who tells it. I'm for justice, no matter who it's for or against" -Malcolm X

Think of a loved one you have lost. I'm sure you remember their face, or a particularly memorable event you shared. You may remember their home, car or clothes and at some point you will probably think of an adjective that describes something about them.

"Grandma was a *fabulous* cook, grandpa was a *kind* man," or, "uncle Allan was a *bad* drunk."

But you don't remember them as that adjective. That is just one description of the deep and entangled web of attributes that was your loved one. Grandma may have been a fabulous cook, but she was possibly really bad at social media. So it may not be accurate to remember her as strictly fabulous. Her clothes or politics may not meet the same criteria as her cooking. Even if you do think of your loved one as fabulous, you most certainly don't call them that adjective as their name. You don't say, "I miss Fabulous Grandma."

But Ivan Vasilyevich's adjective not only describes almost the whole of his person, but it also became his name. His actions have defined him for centuries, replacing his full name with an adjective in English, and that adjective is terrible.

Ivan the Terrible

By 1543 Ivan had witnessed the torture of countless people. His own uncle Yuri, who challenged Ivan's birthright to the throne, was tossed in a dungeon and starved to death. His mother, Jelena Glinsky, died suddenly after allegedly ordering the execution of other family members. Historians believe it was poisoning, administered by angered relatives of murdered opponents. Within a week of her death, Prince Ivan

Obolensky was beaten to death by his jailers for his loyalty to Glinsky. A feud between the Shuisky family and the Belsky family resulted in more torture and murder. During this time historians believe Ivan was molested and beaten regularly. He resorted to torturing animals by throwing them off roofs, gouging out their eyes and other barbaric acts.

Finally, on December 29, 1543, Ivan ordered Prince Andrew Shuisky arrested and executed. He had Shuisky thrown to a pack of starving dogs. This was the symbolic beginning of Ivan's reign over Russia.

He was 13.

Eventually, Ivan instituted the Oprichniki to "manage" his people. These were groups of men, dressed in black, with a sworn oath to Ivan. They were little more than a murderous gang roaming the country with the blessing and protection of a paranoid and delusional dictator. They claimed holy authority as they tortured and murdered priests in front of congregations and performed torture, rape and theft at will They had the permission, and at times, personal assistance of Ivan. Their orders were to eliminate anyone not loyal to Ivan. Unfortunately disloyalty was much easier to prove, than loyalty.

It was nothing for Ivan and the Oprichniki to have people drawn over powder kegs and blown up, tortured and murdered in front of their families and boiled or skinned alive.

In one story, Ivan and the Oprichniki had a peasant stripped naked and used her as target practice. Ivan's weapon of choice was a staff with a pointed, metal, spear tip affixed to the top. This would be the spear that, in a fit of rage, he ran through the skull of his favorite son, killing him. The death was the culmination of an argument that came about because Ivan had beaten his pregnant daughter-in-law and caused the miscarriage of his own grandchild during a prior fit of rage. Daniel von Bruchau described Ivan during these fits saying he, "foamed at the mouth like a horse."

At one point a peasant approached Ivan and rebuked him for not paying attention during church. So Ivan did something unthinkable.

He sat up and paid attention in church.

Allow me to repeat that. Ivan, who thought nothing of committing horrible acts to clergy, during church, in front of the congregation, and who used peasants as target practice, is approached by a peasant in church. The peasant does the modern equivalent of grabbing Ivan by the ear tells him to sit up straight and pay attention, and Ivan does.

In fact, not only does Ivan listen, he sends the peasant a gift, which the peasant gives away publicly!

In one anecdote, this same pauper engages Ivan during Lent, in which observers, including Ivan, abstained from meat. As he approached Ivan at dinner and dropped a large piece of bloody meat on the table in front of Ivan. Ivan explained that he did not eat meat during Lent. The peasant said, "You eat and drink the blood and flesh of those you kill and torture." In other words, "Ivan, you are so deplorable, that eating this steak during Lent is not really going to matter when it comes to your salvation."

How did Ivan react? By acting as a pallbearer at this mans funeral years later, when he died of natural causes. It was plainly obvious that Ivan loved, and listened to this man. In fact, it seems that this person had carte blanche when it came to speaking into Ivan's life, more so than any other person.

If you visit Moscow today, just outside the Kremlin stands a beautiful building. It's oversized domes and intricate paint scheme makes the building stand out as a unique, worldwide treasure. Much like the Taj Mahal, most people have seen it in pictures because it is one of the most photographed pieces of architecture in the world.

It's design is best describes as a bonfire. Dmitry Shvidkovsky, in his book *Russian Architecture and the West*, writes, "it is like no other Russian building. Nothing similar can be found in the entire millennium of Byzantine tradition from the fifth to fifteenth century ... a strangeness that astonishes by its unexpectedness, complexity and dazzling interleaving of the manifold details of its design."

It's name is St. Basils Cathedral, named after the pauper who had so much influence over Ivan, Vasily Blazhenny or simply, Basil.

At the age of 13, (oddly the same age as Ivan when he ordered his first execution) Basil dedicated his life to Christ and remained for over 70 years. He wore very little clothing, even during the harsh Russian winters. He had an incredible sense of passion, lived in the moment and opened the doors to a much deeper and higher sense of worship than those around him. He was not typical, but he fit the description of a very small group of people throughout history who acted similarly. They were called, "The Holy Fools of Russia," and they seemed to have something that others did not.

So what did Basil have that made him so dedicated, so passionate and so influential? How could a man, with almost none of the typical makings of stature in his culture, who spoke so bluntly, become revered and beloved by the tyrant who murdered his own son?

Some historians believe Basil had an incredible brain anomaly that caused him to act the way he did. People affected by this anomaly have a surplus of synapses, or connections between brain cells. This happens when the natural pruning of these synapses which usually takes place in our brain, doesn't occur the way it should. It has many symptoms and causes different results in the people it affects. Historically it has gone by many different names.

But today it is most simply know as autism.

John Donavan and Caren Zucker explained this rationale in their bestselling book, In a Different Key, The Story of Autism. The following is an excerpt.

-Half a millennium ago, a Russian shoemaker named Basil, born around 1469, was spotted walking about naked in winter, spouting incomprehensible utterances, while remaining inattentive to his own needs, even for food. The populace did not see this as madness. They thought, rather, that they were witnessing extreme holiness. The Russians called this "foolishness for Christ" and reared Basil's self-abnegation as courageous, difficult, and a pious path, which Basil took in order to allow Christ to speak through him. Even the tsar-Ivan the Terrible- who was known to have waiters executed for serving the wrong drink at dinner, let Basil criticize him in public. He believed Basil could read his thoughts, and he took it to heart when the wandering shoemaker scolded him for letting his mind wander in church. It was said that Basil was the only man Ivan truly feared.

In 1974, a pair of Russian-speaking scholars at the University of Michigan suggested that something other than pure foolishness or holiness might have been at work in Basil, and in a few others with similar stories. Natalia Challis and Horace Dewey dove deeply into the available accounts of Basil's life and some thirty-five other "Holy Fools" of bygone days, all recognized as saints by the Russian Orthodox Church. Challis's and Dewey's academic specialty was Russian history and culture, not autism. But Dewey had a son, born in the 1950's who had been diagnosed with autism, and that gave him insights into the behaviors of the ancient wanderers. He came to believe that autism, not insanity or divinity, might explain the Holy Fools' behavior.

This set of individuals, he and Challis wrote, were "unhampered by society's preconceptions" and content to live in a state of social isolation. Certain of them were wedded to rituals. They noted that Basil's tolerance of extreme cold-which let him "walk barefoot on the frozen Volga"- was reminiscent of how some people with autism appear indifferent to extremes of cold, heat, or pain. The Holy Fools were also observed to get by on limited sleep and food-again, similar to some people with autism.

While some remained mute, several were known to echo the words of others, and still others spoke in riddles. And legend has it that some blurted out what they were thinking into the faces of the powerful. That tendency, Challis and Dewey wrote, was a major part of what endeared the Fools to the Russian public. In a culture where few dared to question authority, their impertinence was reminiscent of the great prophets of the Old Testament.-

Was autism the secret tool Basil used to influence one of the most horrible people that lived? Could the personality of those on the autism spectrum lend itself, in some ways, to persuasion and influence? If you are considering a person you know with autism, and you are realizing that some of the traits they exhibit do seem persuasive, you are not wrong.

In July of 2017, verywell.com published their Top 10 Positive Traits of Autistic People. The article garnered some negative reviews because of the generalization of people on the spectrum. People with autism are referred to as being on the autism spectrum because autism results in set of personal characteristics somewhat different from what we consider average. But not every person with autism has all of the characteristics listed on the spectrum.

For example some of the characteristics on the spectrum are as follows:

- Intense or focused interests
- Repetitive body movements such as spinning or hand flapping
- Unusual sensory interests such as sniffing objects or staring intently at moving objects
- Insistence on sticking to routines
- Sensory sensitivities including avoidance of everyday sounds and textures

(You can learn more at autismspectrum.org.au)

Though these are a few of the behaviors on the spectrum, not every person with autism will exhibit all of these behaviors. While Down Syndrome is quantifiable; every person it affects has an extra chromosome, autism is not. For example a person with autism may insist on routines, but might not show repetitive body movements. Because the range of behaviors can be so varied, the term "autism spectrum" is used to describe the set of possible behaviors of an autistic person.

But the people at verywell.com believe that most people on the spectrum share a common set of endearing characteristics. They are:

1. People with autism rarely lie
2. People on the autism spectrum live in the moment
3. People with autism rarely judge others
4. People on the spectrum are passionate
5. People with autism are not tied to social expectations
6. People with autism have terrific memories
7. People on the spectrum are less materialistic
8. People with autism play fewer head games
9. People on the autism spectrum have fewer hidden agendas
10. People with autism open new doors for neurotypicals

These are obviously not scientific explanations or descriptions of people with autism. But anecdotally, I think it's fair to say the people on the spectrum whom I have met do live up to this high praise. Think of it. Frequently someone on the spectrum will say things that seem socially inappropriate, but it is usually inappropriate because it is awkwardly true and said passionately without judgement. Just simply a momentary fact, most of us wouldn't say. They call neurotypicals on our facades at times and in places we would never dream of. This very common trait associated with autism is the embodiment of numbers 1, 2, 3, 5, 9 and 10 from the list. It is hard to argue these traits and, when shown in the proper light, these traits are endearing.

Most of the items on the list are really just personality traits many of us would love to have more of. We can all play fewer head games or judge others less. It seems at least some of these positive traits describe a personality that is not only attainable, but influential. An honest, non-judgmental, passionate person with no hidden agenda who plays fewer head games than the average person is someone to whom I am likely to listen.

Is the personality verywell.com describes also common in influencers? Is their list a little-known set of characteristics that inherently reside with those on the autism spectrum? Are those characteristics integral in ethical persuasion or principled influence?

Were these the keys to Basil's personality that put him in such high regard in the eyes of the serial sadist, Ivan?

And just how pivotal is personality when it comes to persuasion and influence? What mattered more, who Basil was or what he said and did?

A huge portion of potential influencers spend mountains of time finessing the message, campaign or product, and less time developing the personality of the influencer or messenger. In my opinion this is a huge mistake. That the message, campaign or product has to be high-quality and good for the audience should be a given. But focusing on small details around the product or message is a mistake if the messenger doesn't resonate with the audience.

In the incredible book Blink, by Malcolm Gladwell, he unequivocally proved, at least to me, that the personality of the messenger is not only pivotal, but actually has more to do with influence than the messages themselves. I arrived at this conclusion when Gladwell described the real reasons doctors are sued for medical malpractice. And it has much less to do with medical malpractice than we think.

Gladwell writes, "The overwhelming number of people who suffer an injury due to the negligence of a doctor never file a malpractice suit at all. Patients don't file lawsuits because they've been harmed by shoddy medical care. Patients file lawsuits because they've been harmed by shoddy medical care – and something else happens to them."

He continues,

-Recently the medical researcher Wendy Levinson recorded hundreds of conversations between a group of physicians and their patients. Roughly half of the doctors had never been sued. The other half had been sued at least twice, and Levinson found that just on the basis of those conversations, she could find clear differences between the two groups.

The surgeons who had never been sued spent more than three minutes longer with each patient than those who had been sued did (18.3 minutes versus 15 minutes). They were more likely to make "orienting" comments, such as "First I'll examine you, and then we will talk the problem over" or "I will leave time for your questions" – which help patients get a sense of what the visit is supposed to accomplish and when they ought to ask questions. They were more likely to engage in active listening, saying things such as "Go on, tell me more about that," and they were far more likely to laugh and be funny during the visit."

Interestingly, there was no difference in the amount or quality of information they gave their patients; they didn't provide more details about medication of the patient's condition. The difference was entirely in how they talked to their patients.-

In a nutshell, the personality of the doctors determined if the patient would sue them for medical malpractice, not the quality of care. Gladwell goes on to explain situations where patients wanted to sue because they felt they were given inadequate care. But when they realized the suit would hurt the people in the office whom they liked, they chose not to continue.

This is the power of personality. It is the engine that drives influence. It is a measuring stick by which most of us gauge the degree of influence we allow someone to have in our lives. We do not accurately evaluate every decision, purchase or vote and come up with rational choices. In the context of influence, the personality of the influencer is what researchers call a heuristic. Heuristics are gauges, or rules of thumb that we have gathered to make processing information easier, and often they are very often wrong.

In Richard Thaler's book Misbehaving, he explains some of these mistakes in practical, real life, economical examples. He explains that a man who suffers from hay fever mows his own lawn. When asked why he doesn't hire a kid from the neighborhood to mow the lawn for $10 the man says it isn't worth it. In other words he would rather save $10 by mowing a lawn and suffering through the hay fever.

So, in logical, analog terms, hay fever is worth $10 to that man. But when he is asked if he would mow a different lawn of roughly the same size for $20 the man says absolutely not. But this thinking is irrational. If hay fever is worth $10 to the man then it should definitely be worth $20.

But the man is reacting to a heuristic that behavioral analysts call loss aversion. As a rule we over-value what we already have to very inaccurate results. The man with hay fever is valuing the $10 he is saving more than the $20 he would earn mowing the other lawn.

Loss aversion is an example of an irrational heuristic that influences most people. But these heuristics, irrational or not, are usually the guardrails of our decisions. They offer us the ability to make decisions in multiple contexts.

But context can often change the heuristic.

Imagine I approach you in a shopping mall and ask your help with a math question. You agree to help, so I present the following problem. There are two pieces of railroad track, each one is a mile long, laid end to end. The tracks are secured at each end and touch in the middle. The railroad tracks each expand by one inch, into each other lifting the middle in the air. Also imagine they do not flex. Instead they are perfectly rigid, forming a triangle with the ground as the base. Here is the question, how high do the tracks raise?

The average guess is two inches. Each track expands an inch and there are two tracks so two inches. Most people use the information readily available as a heuristic, make a guess and move on.

Now suppose you are in a geometry class. The topic is pythagorean theorem or the measurements of right triangles. The teacher explains that any triangle with two equal legs can be divided into two right triangles by drawing a line from the point of the triangle to the center of the hypotenuse. The newly drawn line can be measured by applying the pythagorean theory to each triangle as long as you know the length of the other two legs. Then she explains the same problem a different way. The leg of a right triangle is 5280' or one mile long. The hypotenuse of the same triangle is 5280'1", one mile and one inch. She hands you a calculator and asks, "what is the length of the other leg?"

Now the context is different but the problem is the same. You have the formula and you have a calculator. In just a few seconds you arrive at the right answer, which is 29.6 ft. Notice that the average answer of two inches is way off. The heuristics or rules of thumb we use in the absence of all of the information is often extremely wrong.

Because the context of the mall scenario is so different than the classroom, even people who know the pythagorean theory, and have a calculator on the phone in their pocket, get the answer wrong. Most of us would need to be in the presence of the right context in order to arrive at the right choice, even if we have access to all of the necessary information. But most of our decisions and choices are made in the a context lacking complete information. Which is why the personality of the influencer usually affects the choice of the majority of consumers more than facts or data.

When we cast our vote we don't usually do it with a full set of information. Typically our logic goes something like this, "I am a gun-owner and he supports the NRA," or, "I have glaucoma and she supports medical marijuana." We don't think in actual terms like, "She supports medical marijuana, unless Congress has been overwhelmingly filled with right-wing candidates on the back of a huge growth of Christianity and she thinks the constituents are moving away from supporting legalized medical marijuana." That is foolish. We assign people fundamental attributes and assume those attributes span every situation.

We say, "Thomas is kind." We don't say, "Thomas is kind, unless he didn't sleep all night, and the barista is rude and messes up his order." This is called the fundamental attribution error. It is a heuristic or rule of thumb that we use to make decisions in multiple contexts to make our life easier. It would be impossible to go into every decision armed with all of the information about that situation. So in our day to day dealings with people, we assign fundamental attributions to them. If the messenger attracts poor fundamental attributions, it won't matter what the message is.

Heuristics and context are why the personality of the influencer is so critical.

Book purchases are a perfect example. People do not buy books because of the information in them. If that were true then people would need to read the book before they buy it to find out if the information is worth paying for. People buy books based on their view of the author, or the personality of the friend who recommended it, or the context of their need and the answer promised by the cover. But no one purchases a book because they have read it and evaluated the information first, and then choose to buy it. Hardly any influence is made in that manner. The personality of the messenger and context of the situation almost always holds sway over influence and persuasion.

So when the message, product or candidate is a decent choice, the consumer uses context and the personality of the influencer to make their choices. If we spend our time polishing and honing the product or message, but we get the messenger wrong, it won't matter. People choose influencers using heuristics, context and fundamental attributions, not spec sheets and charts.

Incredibly, history has proven some of the traits from the list to be pivotal in creating that influential messenger. Our ideas can only spread when they are offered by someone whose personality of positive fundamental attributions, can build a heuristic of trust and create the context in which influence grows.

In SWAY we will dissect a few of the personality traits on the list of positive attributes of people on the autism spectrum. We will look back at history and find people who had the opportunity at influence. In each section we will explore one person who used a trait from the list to exercise influence, and one person lacking the trait, who was unable to leave their mark.

Understand that when we study someone with influence, it won't necessarily mean these were people who advanced society. In some cases the most influential people used a trait, or the science behind the trait, to influence humanity for the worse.

Influence is not always positive. We will explore a wide variety of influencers, the traits and science they used and how much influence they actually had.

We will focus on six of the traits, out of order, which I found to be common in the history of influence. They are:

#4 People with autism are passionate
#3 People with autism rarely judge others
#8 People with autism play fewer head games
#5 People with autism are not tied to social expectations
#2 People on the autism spectrum live in the moment
and #10 People with autism open new doors for neurotypicals

We will look closer at a man who had every opportunity to save an immeasurable number of babies and their mothers. His passion and use of it had everything to do with the amount of influence he had. We will look at a businessman who acted completely contrary to the world around him, and what effect it had. We will dive deep in the world of psychopaths and determine the degree of their influence and what science tells is so effective and ineffective about their persuasion.

We will recount the story of one of the originators of the concept of the atom. What trait on the autism spectrum did he use and how was it received?

We will look closely into the terrorist attacks on September 11th, the psychology that led up to the attack and how it could've been avoided.

Plus we will explore how one person single-handedly caused the fall of a 230+ year old bank that, up to that point, had survived WWI, WWII, the French Revolution, the Napoleonic Wars and financed the Louisiana purchase. We will learn how that person, exploiting one trait from the autism spectrum, caused the collapse of the bank that held the Queen's money.

And that isn't all.

History is ripe with examples of successful and failed influencers. The personality of the influencers seems to be the common denominator in the amount of persuasion each person had. What's more, the specific parts of their personality that had the most effect on their influence, seem to fit within the six characteristics from the autism spectrum that we are examining.

My hope is that SWAY will do four things.

1. Help you sniff out the charlatans and crooks who try to coerce influence by manipulating one or more of the traits, or the science behind the trait.
2. Spread the idea that it is more important and effective to develop the messenger, than to manipulate the message.

3. Help you have more influence for the positive changes you are trying to make.
4. (Perhaps most important) Shine a different light on those with autism.

We consider 16th century Russia a brutal and barbaric place. But were they ahead of us when it comes to their view of autism? Did they know something we have forgotten?

Let's find out.

Section 1: Charisma And The Art of Spreading Passion

(People With Autism Are Passionate)

Chapter 1
influence failed

"A great hero, a great truth, a great mission, and finally a mad flight of passionate arrogance resulting in destruction."

"On March 20, 1849 Ignaz Semmelweis was removed from his position in the lying-in department."

This sentence appears lazily at the bottom of page 355 in a book named Medicine: Volume 5 by Harold Nicolas Moyer, as if it didn't matter. But it was everything to dying babies and their mothers.

The book is written in the type of century-old English that made use of big words and long sentences, adding unnecessary length and boredom to otherwise insightful and easily read prose such as the current sentence, of which you are reading. But for some reason it appears so quickly and indistinctly that it seems unimportant. It is almost a footnote.

But, it is far from a footnote. The reason for the "removal" of Ignaz Semmelweis had repercussions that sounded around the world.

Dr. Semmelweis came into his own at a time when medicine was undergoing a massive shift in thinking. The ideas of evil spirits and spells cast by sorcerers as a reason for illness was giving sway to the scientific process. Examination, evaluation and training were slowly gaining favor. It was a virtual ground zero for the medical profession as we know it today.

The complete inexperience and misunderstanding of the medical community then seems ridiculous to us now. But they did not benefit from the trial and error equation of over a century and a half as we do. Medicine then did not have the second, most important part of the equation to study; error.

For instance, Mrs. Winslow's Soothing Syrup was a concoction manufactured by Jeremiah Curtis and Benjamin Perkins of Maine. The two are told to have gotten the recipe from Charlotte Winslow, who was Jeremiah's mother-in-law. She "developed" the wonder drug while she was a nurse herself. She found the mix to be an absolute wonder drug for the infants for whom she cared.

It would instantly soothe and treat even the most inconsolable child, regardless of the ailment. The medicine was a huge hit and in 1868 the company reported to have sold around 1.5 million bottles annually. It seemed the drug worked wonders for relieving pain in infants and stress in parents. Maybe because of its primary ingredient,

65mg per fluid ounce of morphine in every bottle!

Morphine! The same stuff they give to wounded soldiers and terminal cancer patients. The medicine didn't just offer a small hint of morphine either.

Consider this comment by NurseLoey on drugs.com about doses of morphine. "I am a hospice nurse and the standard dose of liquid morphine to keep a pt comfortable is 5mg every 2 hours as needed for pain or shortness of breath."

This from a nurse who treats fully grown patients in the most excruciating time of most of their lives. But Mrs. Winslow was pumping 65mg per ounce medicine into babies on a regular basis.

In 1911 the American Medical Association wrote a book called Nostrums And Quackery, Articles on the Nostrum Evil and Quackery. It is basically an outing of all scams and cons that the AMA could research from sorcery to mail fraud. One sickening section called Baby Killers is exactly what it says. In it, Mrs. Winslow's "remedy" was ripped to shreds. But, being in the experimental and untrained medical environment, it wasn't pulled from the shelves for 19 years after the publication.

Another remedy, indicative of our medical knowledge during the 1800's was Laudanum, which was initially given as a cough suppressant. But, because of it's incredibly addictive qualities, it was actually used to treat almost every conceivable ailment except death.

In Dr. Chase's Recipes, written by Dr. A.W. Chase in 1874, he offers a recipe for making laudanum, in case the lay person wanted to make their own.

Laudanum- Best Turkey opium, 1oz.; slice, and pour upon it boiling water, 1 gill (1/4 pint), and work it in a bowl or mortar until it is dissolved; then pour it into the bottle, and with alcohol of 76 per cent 1/2 pt. (side note, the alcohol recommended in this recipe of 76 per cent, which apparently pairs perfectly with your opium, is a higher percentage of alcohol than almost every liquor available in your neighborhood grocery store, including the famed Bacardi 151.) Rinse the dish, adding the alcohol to the preparation, shaking well and in 24 hours it will be ready for use.

Vin Mariani was a "stomach stimulant, pain reliever and appetite suppressant" sold around the same time. It was made from 6mg of cocaine and 17% alcohol per ounce. Angela Mariani, the Corsican scientist who made the concoction had testimonials from HG Wells, Jules Vern, Thomas Edison, the King of Spain and President William McKinley.

It was a knock-off of Vin Mariana made by John Pemberton, that included a *higher* amount of cocaine which eventually became Coca-Cola.

This was the world in which Dr. Ignaz Semmelweis entered to save lives and advance the fledgling profession of medicine. At the time Puerperal Fever, better known as childbed fever, was killing patients at a rate close to that of some lung cancers today. These were not patients with terminal illness, they were pregnant mothers and the babies they were delivering. In some cases hospitals faced a 50% mortality rate during the childbed (puerperal) fever epidemic. Mothers and babies were dying at alarmingly high rates even by century and a half old standards. Surviving a trip to the hospital was not a common occurrence. Then it happened.

On March 13, 1847 professor Jakob Kolletschka, a contemporary of Semmelweis, died from an infection in his finger. To drive the point home let me write that again.

He died from an infection in his finger!

Dr. Semmelweis noticed some amazing similarities between the pyemia, or blood poisoning, in the professor and the infections of the victims of childbed fever. The similarities convinced him that the infections were coming from passing "poisons from the dead bodies." In other words, death was traveling from the dead or dying patients, on the hands of the staff, to the living and infecting them.

Two months later in May, Semmelweis instituted a rule that before any examinations, doctors or nurses must wash their hands with a chloride of calcium solution. This one change immediately dropped childbed fever deaths by nearly 70%. In October Semmelweis realized that the tools were also spreading death. Again he instituted a rule that mandated tool cleaning in between examinations. This caused the death rate to spiral downwards towards zero.

As a result the numbers get astounding. By March of 1848, 276 women were admitted to a Vienna hospital without a single death for the first time in years.

The hand and tool washing was a complete success, and Semmelweis was its champion. To the 276 women who lived through March of 1848, Semmelweis was literally a lifesaver.

So why is it that one year later Semmelweis was, *"removed from his position in the lying-in department?"* Was it that his life-saving technique didn't include the standard doses of opium, heroin or cocaine for the time? Was there a sinister plot to control the population of the world? Or is the answer even simpler than that?

One likely answer to why Semmelweis was fired has been beautifully demonstrated in a psychological experiment done 120 years later, with toy robots and seven to nine year old boys.

Jonathan Freedman is a very popular name in the anti-child-spanking community of parents. If you dig into the research behind the movement even briefly, you will find his name and this study cited repeatedly. Because Freedman didn't study how to change a child's behavior in the moment. He studied how to influence lasting change, which was the same goal Semmelweis had.

Freedman knew that in 1965 most boys of seven to nine years obeyed their parents as a result of the threat of spanking. Spanking was the gold standard of parenting then. There was not an anti-child-spanking community, in fact it was just the opposite.

Consider this Sunday Dec. 12, 1965 article in the Chicago Tribune titled Princess Grace Does the Spanking in Monaco.

-In a rare interview with this reporter, Princess Grace discussed how she raised her family.

"Children need much love and affection," she said, "but also some discipline. "I'm rather severe with mine."

Did Rainier ever apply a hairbrush to his offspring like ordinary father's?

"Well, sometimes I use my hand on them," she replied.

"Prince Albert," his mother said, "already is being taught that it will be his duty one day to govern the principality," and she added: "It is fairly easy to teach him. He is quiet, and thinks a lot."-

He is quiet, and thinks a lot. Any parent of a toddler knows what a relief those moments of silence can be. The article is not asking about the validity of spanking or if the family used spanking, but how did the family use spanking and who did it.

In the fractured era of Churchill's death, LBJ's Great Society, the start of the Vietnam War, the assassination of Malcolm X and the racial tensions in the American South with Dr. Martin Luther King leading the charge, the validity of spanking was not on the forefront of societal happenings. The quick peace and quiet it brought, much like Mrs. Winslow's Soothing Syrup must have been a huge relief.

But the small experiment I mentioned earlier, happening in the backdrop of this pivotal moment in history, would go on to influence the parenting style of the nation and, at the same time, explain why Dr. Semmelweis was fired a century earlier.

This excerpt from Readings in Managerial Psychology by M. Boje explains it best.

-An experiment by Jonathan Freedman gives us some hints about what to do and what not to do in this regard.

Freedman wanted to see if he could prevent second to fourth grade boys from playing with a fascinating toy, just because he had said that it was wrong to do so some six weeks earlier. Anyone familiar with seven to nine year old boys must realize the enormity of the task. But Freedman had a plan. If he could first get the boys to convince themselves that it was wrong to play with the forbidden toy, perhaps that belief would keep them from playing with it thereafter. The difficult thing was making the boys believe that it was wrong to amuse themselves with the toy-an extremely expensive, battery controlled robot. (This was in 1965)

Freedman knew it would be easy enough to have a boy obey temporarily. All he had to do was threaten the boy with severe consequences should he be caught playing with the toy. As long as he was nearby to deal out stiff punishment, Freedman figured that few boys would risk operating the robot. He was right. After showing a boy an array of five toys and warning him, "It is wrong to play with the robot. if you play with the robot I'll be very angry and will have to do something about it," Freedman left the room for a few minutes. During that time, the boy was observed secretly through a one-way mirror. Freedman tried this threat procedure on twenty-two different boys, and twenty-one of them never touched the robot while he was gone.

So a strong threat was successful while the boys thought they might be caught and punished. But Freedman had already guessed that. He was really interested in the effectiveness of the threat in guiding the boys' behavior later on, when he was no longer around. To find out what would happen then he sent a young woman back to the boys' school about six weeks after he had been there. She took the boys out of the class one at a time to participate in an experiment. Without ever mentioning any connection with Freedman, she escorted each boy back to the room with the five toys and gave him a drawing test. While she was scoring the test, she told the boy that he was free to play with any toy in the room. Of course, almost all the boys played with a toy. The interesting result was that, of the boys playing with a toy, 77 percent chose to play with the robot that had been forbidden to them earlier. Freedman's severe threat, which had been so successful six weeks before, was almost totally unsuccessful when he was no longer able to back it up with punishment.

But Freedman wasn't finished yet. He changed his procedure slightly with a second sample of boys. These boys, too, were initially shown the array of five toys by Freedman and warned not to play with the robot while he was briefly out of the room because, "it is wrong to play with the robot." But this time, Freedman provided no strong threat to frighten a boy into obedience. He simply left the room and observed through the one-way mirror to see if his instruction against placing with the forbidden toy was enough. It was. Just as with the other sample, only one of the twenty-two boys touched the robot during the short time Freedman was gone.

The real difference between the two samples of boys came six weeks later, when they had a chance to play with the toys while Freedman was no longer around. An astonishing thing happened with the boys who had earlier been given no strong threat against playing with the robot. When given the freedom to play with any toy they wished, most avoided the robot, even though it was by far the most attractive of the five toys available (the others were a cheap plastic submarine, a child's baseball glove without a ball, an unloaded toy rifle, and a toy tractor.) When these boys played with one of the five toys, only 33 percent chose the robot.

Something dramatic had happened to both groups of boys. For the first group, it was the severe threat they heard from Freedman to back up his statement that playing with the robot was "wrong." It had been quite effective at first, while Freedman could catch them. Should they violate his rule later, though, when he was no longer present to observe the boys' behavior, his threat was impotent and his rule was, consequently, ignored. It seems clear that the threat had not taught the boys that operating the robot was wrong, only that it was unwise to do so when the possibility of punishment existed.

For the other boys, the dramatic event had come from the inside, not the outside. Freeman had instructed them, too, that playing with the robot was wrong, but he had added no threat of punishment should they disobey him. There were two important results. First, Freedman's instruction alone was enough to prevent the boys from operating the robot while he was briefly out of the room. Second, the boys took personal responsibility for their choice to stay away from the robot during that time. They decided that they hadn't played with it because they didn't want to. After all, there were no strong punishments associated with the toy to explain their behavior otherwise. Thus, weeks later, when Freedman was nowhere around, they still ignored the robot because they had been changed inside to believe the they did not want to play with it.-

With that study, Freedman proved, at least in young boys playing with robots, forcing them to act a certain way did not change their minds about acting that way. Threats only created the desirable situation in the moment, but it did not create lasting change. In fact, a natural, psychological reaction that we all experience probably had the opposite effect from Freedman's demands. This natural occurrence is called psychological reactance.

One definition of psychological reactance explains it this way.

Psychological Reactance is a motivational reaction to offers, persons, rules, or regulations that threaten or eliminate specific behavioral freedoms. Reactance occurs when a person feels that someone or something is taking away their choices or limiting the range of alternatives.

In other words, we are much less likely to do something that someone tells us to do, or threatens our freedoms for, than if someone just asks. Almost none of us respond well to threats, because of psychological reactance, and there is science to back it up.

In a Quick and Stephenson 2008 study, they proved that dogmatic language initiated psychological reactance. The following are examples of that language.

1. Imperatives such as must or need.

2. Absolute allegations, such as cannot deny that or this issue is extremely serious.

3. Derision towards other perspectives, such as any reasonable person would agree that.

We can see that demands get us the opposite of what we are after. In contrast, messages that are less dogmatic do not provoke psychological reactance such as.

1. Allusions to choice such as you have the chance to or we leave the choice to you.

2. Qualified propositions such as there is some evidence that their issue is fairly serious.

3. Avoidance of imperatives or derisive language. Rather than saying, "Take out the trash," say, "Please take out the trash."

Psychological reactance may explain, very clearly what happened to Dr. Semmelweis and his cleanliness initiative, if you understand the type of man Semmelweis was.

Not much is written about the firing of Dr. Semmelweis except a few scattered sentences like the one at the beginning of this chapter. But his angry and abusive personality is well documented. For the most part, his disposition has been surmised as the reason for his termination.

It is widely accepted that he forced and threatened his sanitation practices into existence. Sherwin B. Nunland captured the personality of Semmelweis using the doctor's own words in his book Doctors: The Biography of Medicine.

Here is an excerpt.

"To Josef Spaeth, Professor of Obstetrics at the Josefs-Akademie of the University of Vienna, he (Semmelweis) wrote:

-Herr Professor, you have convinced me that the Puerperal Sun which arose in Vienna in the year 1847 has not enlightened your mind even though it shone so near to you . . . . .This arrogant ignoring of my doctrine, this arrogant boasting about errors, demands that I make the following declaration: Within myself, I bear the knowledge that since the year 1847 thousands and thousands of puerperal women and infants who have died would not have died had I not kept silent, instead of providing the necessary correction to every error that has been spread about puerperal fever . . . . And you, Herr Professor, have been a partner in this massacre.-

To Friedrich Scanzoni, Professor of Obstetrics at Wurzburg, who admittedly was wrong about hand washing, but advanced the medical practice by leaps in his life, Semmelweis wrote:

-Should you, Herr Professor, without having disproved my doctrine, continue to train your pupils with the doctrine of epidemic childbed fever, I declare before God and the world that you are a murderer and the "History of Childbed Fever" would not be unjust to you if it memorialized you as a medical Nero.-

The book goes on to explain that Semmelweis never saw himself as anything but an outsider. He came from a humble background, did not read or write nearly as well as his counterparts and did not have the confidence to stand up to any criticism. His lack of charisma and confidence coupled with his anger and arrogance would steal his opportunity to influence the world.

It wasn't until 1867 when a man named Joseph Lister, of Listerine fame, showed up and actually began influencing doctors to wash their tools. If you are keeping track that is 18 years of unnecessary childbed fever deaths.

Between 1849, when Semmelweis was fired, but had proved his hand washing technique and 1867 when Joseph Lister began *influencing* doctors to wash, roughly 584,500 babies died, just in England and Wales.

How many Mother Teresas, Gandhis, scientific breakthroughs and bestsellers did we lose in those 18 years? Not because we didn't want to save them, or didn't know how, but because one man didn't have the right charisma for influence.

It wouldn't be until 1867 that the information Semmelweis worked so hard to get actually saved lives.

But, by then Semmelweis would be dead.

In his later years (which weren't that late) he became more angry, more inappropriate and consumed with bitterness. His writings and actions were a cause for alarm in his family and associates, (it isn't certain if he had many friends.)

In July of 1865, Semmelweis was tricked into visiting an insane asylum in Lazarettgasse. He thought he was going there to look at a patient as a favor to one of his peers. Instead he was to be committed. When the aging doctor caught on, he tried to escape unsuccessfully. The guards caught him, beat him, restrained him and put him in the equivalent of solitary confinement. During the beating he was wounded. Two weeks later, on August 13th, 1865 Ignaz Semmelweis died.

He was only 47.

In a twisted turn of fate, the doctor died from a pyemia or blood poisoning. It was the same fate that had befallen professor Jakob Kolletschka, who died from the infection in his finger, which sparked the hand-washing inspiration in Semmelweis. The pyemia came as a result of a wound he received in the beating.

If the charisma of Dr. Semmelweis had been different, if his personality had been sweeter, would babies have lived? Does passion and influence spread on the wings of charisma?

Think for a moment of someone on the spectrum. Do they command you to sit and listen at length as they describe their obsession or do we instinctively offer them more time because they smile while they talk about it or because it is exciting to them? Spreading passion hinges on the charisma of the messenger. In the next chapter we will look at a man with an incredible knack for charisma, the influence he garnered and how you can apply this to your endeavors.

We are not usually subjects of conspiracy, or fate. We are the recipients of the fruits offered by the life we have chosen to live and perhaps more importantly, by the person we have chosen to become.

The chapter on Semmelweis in Doctors: The Biography of Medicine ends this way.

"And so Sophocles might have written it, with a Greek chorus of dying mothers a great hero, a great truth, a great mission, and finally a mad flight of passionate arrogance resulting in destruction. The gods who were the professors of obstetrics did not bring it about; the hero brought it upon himself."

Section 1: Charisma And The Art of Spreading Passion

(People With Autism Are Passionate)

Chapter 2
influence achieved

"What good fortune for governments that the people do not think."
-Author revealed at the end of this chapter.

Paul Ludwig Hans Anton von Beneckendorff und von Hindenburg looks like he was ready to punch the photographers who took his all of his pictures.

His large square, angry head commands most of the attention in his photos that isn't already taken by his huge, almost cartoon-like mustache. The mustache looks drawn on, and is wider than his massive jaw. Imagine the hero of a movie, battle-tested and often the victor, being called out of retirement again and again, crashing through opportunities to serve his country in its time of need.

This was the life of Hindenburg.

Again and again he would be called out of retirement to serve in one fashion or another.

Hindenburg had a burning dislike for Communism, which drove many of his actions. He was chosen to lead his people often in battle and politics, and his name has gone down in history. His actions and influence sparked a famous, worldwide event and qualified him for the second chapter of this book, but probably not for the reason you think.

To understand just how pivotal Hindenburg was and the influence he had, it is important that we take a look at the Law of Reciprocal Concessions.

If you have ever bought a car from a dealership, the odds are that you have seen the Law of Reciprocal Concession first hand.

The car you want typically has an outrageous sticker price. You have already decided how much you are willing to pay and the price they are asking is way above your price. You decide there is no way you are leaving with that car. There is just too much distance between the price you are willing to pay and the price they are asking, but you pull in anyway.

You learn about the special options, and the limited number of cars in this color in your area, which you know are both sales tactics. After a brief courtship it is time to discuss price.

The salesperson explains that the price is so high because of the special features and limited availability of the car. They know the car will sell for that price but, just for fun, want to know what you are willing to pay.

When they hear your number they are obviously disturbed. The sales manager, who is hiding behind a partition at this point, won't ever let the car go for that price. But the sales person likes you and wants to see you happy, so they'll ask the manager if they can come down on the price.

After what seems like the length of an extended chess game, the sales person comes out, wipes the sweat from their brow and explains they just fought with the manager for you and have good news. They talked the price down It isn't as much as you wanted but it's way more than they expected to get from the stodgy manager.

Enter the Law of Reciprocal Concessions, or the door in the face technique. Robert Cialdini introduced this to me in his fantastic book Influence. In it, he chronicles his experience as he went undercover in the world of persuasion. He worked in many sales capacities and found that there were really only six principles being used in the professions of persuasion, although countless variations and applications. The Law of Reciprocal Concessions is just a segment of a larger technique called the Law of Reciprocity, which we will delve into more. But the segment called reciprocal concessions is so relevant and much more common than most think.

Have you ever been offered a free sample, a trial period, or a free download with no obligation to buy? What the "free" sample actually does is trigger the feeling of being in debt in our brains. Once we are indebted, our brain does horrible things to itself.

In fact Lawrence M. Berger from the University of Wisconsin published a paper in October of 2012 titled "Household Debt and Adult Depressive Symptoms." His conclusion was that more debt was associated with "greater depression and stress, declining quality of marital relations and parenting behavior and adverse child outcomes." To sum it up, debt feels horrible. But don't despair because the feeling of being in debt can usually be shaken by paying off the debt or offering something back to the debtor.

This is exactly what the free trial is designed to make you feel. The sense of indebtedness makes you want to return the favor to the debtor, but the only thing the debtor wants is a sale. And because they have already lost ground by offering you something you want, they have conceded something. So we automatically feel obligated to pay them back with the purchase.

This is why the lady at the big box store stands next to her station and hands out tasty samples, every website offers a free download and car salespeople come out of the office proud to tell you about the "concession" they got from their manager.

The difference is a sample actually lets us decide if we like the product, the free download usually offers a bit of a solution to our problem, with an offer to buy the rest. But the price haggling technique is nothing but psychological trickery from the sales person.

In reality most sales people know exactly what price they can take for each car. I think the "managers" are much like the Wizard of Oz. They are just the person behind a curtain who you rarely see. They are the easy target when the salesperson want to blame someone for bad news.

I have often imagined what happens as the sales person disappears into the abyss of the manager's office. After learning how car sales people have manipulated this technique, I can picture them slapping each other on the back, watching funny YouTube videos and saying, "This law of reciprocal concessions is great! Now watch this kitty video while that poor schmuck outside waits for 20 minutes."

Another version of the misuse of this technique is when a salesperson asks for a sale, usually after an unsolicited contact, gets denied and then asks, "Ok, well if you aren't interested would you mind giving me the name of someone who would be?" We feel pity on the person so we offer a name, (well, **we** don't because **I** immediately begin trying to sell something to any salesperson who makes unsolicited contact with me. They usually leave, irritated.)

But what we didn't know about some of these "salespeople" is that what they wanted all along was another name. Often times these people are building lists to sell to unscrupulous companies who mail, call or email the people on the list for something completely different than the offer made during the initial contact.

After telling someone no, or beating them at the game, most people have no problem giving their counterpart something small in return for the rejection. But scammers and some care sales people, know this and will offer a huge ask or high price in the beginning, just to get to their "concession" which, in the end, they hope you will reciprocate.

Reciprocal concessions was one of many things that pushed Hindenburg to make the choice he made. It would cement him as a part of one of the largest events in recent history, and I am not referring to the blimp that crashed and burned with his name attached, though it was named after him.

On January 30, 1933, Paul von Hindenburg made a concession to his opponent in the previous election. A man whom he had beaten 18,651,497 votes to 11,339,446 in one round of voting and 19,359,983 votes to 13,418,547 in the second bout.

With the defeat still palpable, the politicians around his opponent lobbied Hindenburg to make a concession and appoint Adolf Hitler as Chancellor of Germany. A year and a half later, Hindenburg would have signed the Enabling Act, granting Hitler an extreme amount of unchecked power, and then die. Hitler would take control of Germany and eventually murder over 11 million people.

Was Hindenburg reacting to the Law of Reciprocal Concessions when he made that critical error? I think so. I doubt that he foresaw what Hitler would become. Just a few years earlier, in Time Magazine he said, "all my impressions of war are so bad that I could be for it only under the sternest necessity — the necessity of fighting Bolshevism or of defending one's country," neither of which were the spark of WWII.

But the Law of Reciprocal Concessions is not enough to sell a car, appoint power to your rival or affect influence. Many times the lady offering the free sample frowns and is silent during the exchange, sparking very few sales. Reciprocal Concession does not work alone. It needs a partner, and that partner is charisma. Something Semmelweis was missing, but Hitler had plenty of.

It is hard to imagine Hitler as charismatic. After all, he is the archetypical villain right? A psychotic madman who coerced a country and manipulated a culture into hate and murder couldn't possibly be charismatic, could he?

Emma Mason wrote this, regarding the charisma of Hitler in October 2012 for the BBC's History Magazine.

–Stop for a moment and imagine Adolf Hitler. Picture him in your mind. Who do you see? I imagine you see a figure not unlike the portrayal of Hitler in the film *Downfall* (2004). A shouting, aggressive, unhinged character. Bruno Ganz, who played Hitler in *Downfall*, shook and screamed so much that one key scene from the movie has become an internet phenomenon, with comical subtitles on a host of subjects being set to Ganz's incredible ranting.

But while it's true that in his last days Hitler was at times scarcely rational, it's not representative of the whole history. Moreover, the trouble is that this image plays into a deep desire I think most of us secretly possess. We want Hitler to have been a lunatic from start to finish. We want Hitler to be mad because it makes the monstrous crimes he committed – particularly during the Second World War – easy to explain.

It's simple. We can tell ourselves comfortably, Hitler was a madman who somehow hypnotized millions of ordinary Germans to do things against their better judgment. Well, he wasn't a madman, and he hypnotized no one.

Hitler became chancellor of Germany in January 1933 by democratic means. A large number of the German elite – sharp, clever people – decided to back him. Why would they support a lunatic? And the way Hitler conducted himself between 1930 and 1933 demonstrated that he was an astute – but wholly unscrupulous – politician. His calculations about where power really lay in Germany and how to best manipulate the emotions of ordinary Germans were extremely sophisticated.

In addition, Hitler generated enormous – and genuine – support. His views very often matched those of huge numbers of the German population. That's something incomprehensible if we take at face value the portrayal of Hitler as a screaming nightmare.-

The fact is, monsters aren't elected. People vote for the best parts of their candidates, or the good, likable characteristics that the candidate has chosen to showcase. It is only after the election when the monster shows up.

What people elect is, charisma. The missing element from the personality of Dr. Semmelweis and the aspect of Hitler that the people of Germany followed.

The Germans who elected Hitler were not all murderous thugs who reflected the horrible parts of The Fuhrer. Some, as Emma Mason pointed out, were sharp, clever people, who supported the vision, certainty and hope that Hitler portrayed. These qualities endeared him to a large portion of the German people. Vision, certainty, and endearment were keys to his charisma and influence. The following are English translations of segments of his speeches as examples of each.

Vision
On January 30th, 1937 Hitler made this promise to the German people.

-In the carrying out of the Four Years Plan lies our first task. It will call for gigantic efforts but eventually it will turn out a great blessing for our people. Its purpose is to strengthen our national economic system in all its branches. The execution of it is guaranteed. All those great works which have been started apart from this plan will be continued. Their purpose is to promote the health of the nation and make life more pleasant. Building extensions will be systematically carried out in some of our large cities, as an externalization of the spirit that actuates this great epoch of our national revival. In the forefront of these plans stands that of remodeling and enlarging Berlin and thus making it the real and true metropolis of the German Reich. Therefore I have today appointed, just as I did for the great scheme of national road construction, a general architectural supervisor for Berlin, who is responsible for the reconstruction and extension of the metropolis. Out of the chaos which resulted from the former building schemes in Berlin he will bring order. And that order will be based on such spacious plans as will be worthy of the National Socialist Movement and also of the German metropolis.-

The making of Berlin into a "real and true metropolis" allows his audience to paint any picture of a perfect city in their head. Hitler didn't show them a drawing of the city, he didn't lay out the numbers or the plan for the city. He let his audience paint their own picture. When you cast the vision you never argue with yourself. Hitler knew that if he allowed his listeners to envision their ideals when he spoke, they would attach that ideal to him.

Another way of saying this is, "The broad masses of a population are more amiable to the appeal of rhetoric than to any other force," which is a quote from Hitler.

But why?

Why is casting a vision so powerful in the art of charisma?

Zakary L. Tormala, Jayson S. Jia from Stanford and Michael Norton from the Harvard Business School may have the answer.

The trio published a study on potential vs. accomplishments in the Journal of Personality and Social Psychology in 2012. In the study they completed 8 experiments designed to test whether people preferred accomplishments or potential. The study conclusively found that people support, followed and engage with potential at a much higher rate than with accomplishments.

In other words people often trust what you say you are going to do, more than what you have done.

Here is an example.

In one experiment the group ran Facebook ads for an up-and-coming comedian named Kevin Shea. The ad had four variations of a tag line on the page. The tag lines were;

1. "Critics say he has become the next big thing." (achievement)

2. "Critics say he could become the next big thing." (potential)

3. "Everyone is talking about Kevin Shea." (achievement)

4. "By this time next year, everyone could be talking about Kevin Shea." (potential)

If people clicked on the ad they were offered the opportunity to click on a link labeled "become a fan." The results overwhelmingly proved that people preferred the potential ads much more than the achievement ads. On average, potential frames produced 3.27 times the click-rate and 5.33 times the fan-rate of achievement frames.

The group conducted 7 other experiments with similar results. People, on average, like potential even more than proof, which is why charismatic leaders are great at casting a vision.

Certainty

Hitler had a knack for certainty. In his speech declaring war on the United States of America he said this.

-Deputies! Men of the German Reichstag!

Ever since my peace proposal of July 1940 was rejected, we have clearly realized that this struggle must be fought through to the end. We National Socialists are not at all surprised that the Anglo-American, Jewish and capitalist world is united together with Bolshevism. In our country we have always found them in the same community. Alone we successfully fought against them here in Germany, and after 14 years of struggle for power we were finally able to annihilate our enemies….

Our opponents should not deceive themselves. In the two thousand years of recorded German history, our people have never been more determined and united than today. The Lord of the universe has been so generous to us in recent years that we bow in gratitude before a Providence that has permitted us to be members of such a great nation. We thank Him, that along with those in earlier and coming generations of the German nation, our deeds of honor may also be recorded in the eternal book of German history!-

In an article called How Certainty Transforms Persuasion, Zakary L. Tormala from the above study and Derek D. Rucker explain the four levers of certainty.

Consensus
Repetition
Ease
Defense

In their context they suggest how companies can use these levers to boost certainty. But look how flawlessly Hitler used them in his declaration of war against the US.

Consensus- "Our opponents should not deceive themselves. In the two thousand years of recorded German history, our people have never been more determined and united than today." Two thousand years of Germans have never been more united than today. That's more than consensus. That's a mandate.

Repetition- In the above speech, no less than 5 times Hitler said, "Deputies! Men of the German Reichstag!" This shout was almost like a chant. It was an attention grabber that solidified the idea that Hitler was speaking to his people, the men of the German Reichstag. If you were listening, you were a part of his team.

Ease- "We thank Him (God), that along with those in earlier and coming generations of the German nation, our deeds of honor may also be recorded in the eternal book of German history!" If God is on your side, you should feel at ease about anything you're doing with Him.

Defense-"Ever since my peace proposal of July 1940 was rejected, we have clearly realized that this struggle must be fought through to the end. We National Socialists are not at all surprised that the Anglo-American, Jewish and capitalist world is united together with Bolshevism. In our country we have always found them in the same community. Alone we successfully fought against them here in Germany, and after 14 years of struggle for power we were finally able to annihilate our enemies." People can often defend even the most horrible and inappropriate opinions, when they feel they are under attack.

Endearment.
Unfortunately Hitler's staunch racism endeared him to some his audience.

He said, "What we have to fight for is to ensure existence and increase of our race and our people, the support of our children and the maintenance of the purity of their blood, the freedom and independence of the Fatherland; so that our people may be able to carry out the mission assigned them by the Creator of the universe. Every thought and every idea, every teaching and all learning, must serve this purpose. From this point of view everything is to be tested, and, according to its suitability, either applied or rejected."

Hitler was completely invested in his audience. Notice he did not preach hate for others in this segment. He told millions of Germans that they were Aryans. Despite the ignorance and and hatred in this belief, it connected with the audience and made them feel part of the movement. They were in this together. Even though it was completely wrong, this connection was something that helped cement the charismatic connection between leader and led.

Emil Klein, who heard Hitler speak in the 1920's said this.

"The man gave off such a charisma that people believed whatever he said."

When someone from the spectrum speaks of their passion, often times it's endearing. It is rare when that person can speak of their obsession and not draw you into their conversation. Notice when that person dives into their love, they pull you into their world, and not the other way around. Their passion and charisma can often be magnetic to some degree.

It is so unfortunate that Adolph Hitler had the one thing that Ignaz Semmelweis did not. Imagine the roles reversed. Hitler lacking the charisma to take control of Germany, and Semmelweis smiling at a sea of obstetricians as they washed their hands between deliveries, giving babies the gift of life.

This is the stark contrast of why charisma holds such power in the art of spreading passion. It was not the ideas of the two men that spread or didn't spread. Most humans, when given the equal and evenly presented choice between saving human lives and taking human lives will choose to save them.

But, it was the charisma, or the spreading of the passion behind the two ideas that influenced humanity. Only, in both cases, it was in the wrong direction. Don't worry, in the next section we will explore what happens when good people have influence, and the one trait you can choose today to garner more influence for yourself.

Oh, and you may have guessed the person responsible for the quote at the beginning of this chapter.

"What good fortune for governments that the people do not think." - Adolf Hitler

Section 2 Kindness, The Power Behind Persuasion

(People with Autism Rarely Judge Others)

Chapter 3
influence failed

"If I have seen further than others, it is by standing on the shoulders of giants." -Isaac Newton

The quote above is an inspirational tip of the hat to those predecessors who laid the foundation for our greatest achievements right?

Would you believe the quote is an insult?

What if I told you that this saying, was taken by one of the brightest, most intelligent men to have lived, as a slap in the face?

Would you continue reading?

If I were to explain The Royal Society, the paragraph might be interpreted as the grandiose explosions of an overzealous author who is trying to convince readers that his subject is much bigger than it really is. Rather than fall into that trap, I will let them speak for themselves, with the following three excerpts from their official website royalsociety.org.

-**About Us**

The Society's fundamental purpose, reflected in its founding Charters of the 1660s, is to recognise, promote, and support excellence in science and to encourage the development and use of science for the benefit of humanity.

The Society has played a part in some of the most fundamental, significant, and life-changing discoveries in scientific history and Royal Society scientists continue to make outstanding contributions to science in many research areas.

Income for 2017

In the year to 31 March 2017, the Royal Society's income increased by 10%, from £77.7m to £85.2m. The majority of the Society's income came from grants for charitable activities, which increased by 12% during the year to £64.9m (2016: £58.1m). The Society's core grant from the Department for Business, Energy and Industrial Strategy (BEIS) was £47.2m (2016: £47.1m).
In addition to this, the Society received income from BEIS in respect of £5.5m (2016: £4.0m) in support of the Newton Fund Academies' Programme which aims to develop science and innovation partnerships that promote economic development and social welfare
of partner countries. BEIS also provided a grant to the Society of £4.8m (2016: £mil) under the Global Challenges Research Fund (GCRF), which aims to support cutting-edge research addressing the challenges faced by developing countries.

History

The early years of the Society saw revolutionary advancements in the conduct and communication of science. Hooke's Micrographia and the first issue of Philosophical Transactions were published in 1665 alone. Philosophical Transactions, which established the important concepts of scientific priority and peer review, is now the oldest continuously-published science journal in the world.

We published Isaac Newton's Principia Mathematica, and Benjamin Franklin's kite experiment demonstrating the electrical nature of lightning. We backed James Cook's journey to Tahiti, reaching Australia and New Zealand, to track the Transit of Venus. We published the first report in English of inoculation against disease, approved Charles Babbage's Difference Engine, documented the eruption of Krakatoa and published Chadwick's detection of the neutron that would lead to the unleashing of the atom.

The leading scientific lights of the past four centuries can all be found among the 8,000 Fellows elected to the Society to date. From Newton to Darwin to Einstein and beyond, pioneers and paragons in their fields are elected by their peers. Current Fellows include Jocelyn Bell Burnell, Richard Dawkins, Stephen Hawking and Tim Berners-Lee.-

These excerpts from the site are actually modest, in the opinion of this over zealous author. But with names like Newton, Einstein and Stephen Hawking it's hard to downplay the role they have played in the history of science.

But there is one name that most people overlook when they read this. One person who, in the early days, gave the snowball of science a massive push, but his name is hardly recognized and is passively mentioned in the above description.

Robert Hooke wrote what is possibly the worlds first scientific bestseller. Micrographia (published by the Royal Society in 1665) was literally filled with incredible scientific theories and findings. Through the use of a new technology called the microscope, Robert Hooke was able to describe plant cells, draw intricate drawings of fleas and the eyes of a drone fly. The book doesn't stop at the minuscule though. It deals with distant planets and the light waves. It was a long look through a huge open window of science to all who read it.

It is rumored to have sold all 1,200 copies in one day. To put that in perspective, in 2016 the average book sold less than 250 copies per year and 2000 copies in it's lifetime! over 350 years ago Robert Hooke sold 1,200 in one day, with no internet, no audio books, no bestsellers lists and no publishing agents. This was a massive accomplishment.

But so were the advancements he made to the measurements of time, the pendulum clock, and the pocket watch. He pioneered the balance spring which, coupled with the balance wheel create a harmonic oscillator. This was a revolution in small time pieces and converted them from over-priced tchotchkes to valuable tools for keeping time.

This spring would be at the center of one of his famous feuds.

Christiaan Huyges was a Dutch mathematician and scientist who, nearly a decade after Hooke, claimed to have perfected the pocket watch. This infuriated Hooke because his spring gained very little traction in the previous decade. He claimed to have shown it to the Royal Society, but could not get support to either sell or patent the idea. Now the secretary of the Royal Society, Henry Oldenburg was helping Huygens patent the improvement.

This was salt on an open would for Hooke because Huygens had earlier claimed he had out done Hooke in the creation of a pump. All of this turmoil fell on the backdrop of a disagreement with Hooke had with Johannes Hevelius.

Consider this paragraph from The Amateur Astronomer's Guide to the Deep-Sky Catalogs by Jerry D. Cavin.

-At one point Hevelius became involved in a dispute with Robert Hooke, the English Natural philosopher. The argument concerned Hevelius's observations without the use of a telescope sight and whether they had any scientific value. Hooke learned of Hevelius's methods of using naked-eye observations in the *Machina Coelestis* (1673). The feud between Hevelius and Hooke became so intense that on May 26, 1679, the Royal Society sent a young Edmund Halley to try and resolve the dispute. Upon arrival, Hevelius gave Halley a warm welcome and together they set about planning how to demonstrate the accuracy of Hevelius's naked-eye observations. To perform his measurements Halley used a 2-foot quadrant with telescopic sights. The results of the test were inconclusive. The dispute would continue between Hooke and Hevelius. Although Hooke was right scientifically, and we now recognize that telescopic sights provide far more accurate coordinates than naked-eye observations, the manner in which Hooke expressed himself in the argument did not win him many friends. At the end two of the secretaries of the Royal Society resigned because of the Hooke and Hevelius feud that appeared publicly in the *Philisophical Transactions.-*

Did you catch it? The most collective statement about Hooke, his influence and his persuasion is, "although Hooke was right scientifically…the manner in which Hooke expressed himself in the argument did not win him many friends." This would serve as a mantra for the life and contributions of Robert Hooke.

The story of the brilliant scientist who burst on the community with a bestselling book takes a serious downward spiral at this point. The study of Robert Hooke can scarcely start without the word feud coming up over and over. It seems that, for some reason, people such as Huygens, Henry Oldenburg and Sir Edmund Halley are all happily working to circumvent Hooke.

How is it that one of the most valuable improvements to the pocket watch can be virtually ignored when presented by one man and a decade later the same improvement revolutionize timekeeping when presented by another? How, even in the 1660's could an entire scientific community even entertain the idea that the naked eye was on par with the telescope?

And notice that the Royal Society did not send their famous astrologer, Sir Edmund Halley to work with Hooke, who was of course right. They sent him to work with Hevelius, who was basically licking the tip of his thumb and holding it in the air to study the night sky. How could a man like Hooke be so right on so many fronts and still be shunned by his peers and lost to history?

The answer is balanced or symmetrical reciprocity, another segment of the general law of reciprocity. This natural piece of our psyche seems to be at work in the feuds that litter the life of Hooke.

From his disagreements with little known astronomers and Dutch mathematicians to the biggest feud of his life. The feud that would erase him from history, was not with an obscure thinker, but a household name. It was a person that revolutionized science with whom Hooke finally sparred, and lost. That man was Sir Isaac Newton, and though the psychology of the feud between Newton and Hooke seems to come from balanced or symmetrical reciprocity, history has not been balanced or symmetrical for the two men.

In 1965, an anthropologist named Marshall Sahlins studied reciprocity in humans around the world. In 1965 he claimed that there are three distinct types of reciprocity--generalized, negative and balanced or symmetrical. The following are examples of each.

- Generalized reciprocity is an open-ended offering. For instance, if you help a stranger change a flat tire, you don't finish the transaction with a contract binding that person to help you pull weeds following weekend. We help because we are part of society. If that stranger never returns the favor, it won't stop you from being generous next time. This is a completely altruistic exchange.

- Negative reciprocity is the attempt to get something for nothing. It is the act of taking from society without adding any value in exchange. This is not the person in the above example who is the beneficiary of a kind act. Think Bernie Madoff and other con-men. They are the vacuums of society sucking goodness and trust from the world.

- Balanced or symmetrical reciprocity is tit for tat. Perhaps the best example of balanced reciprocity is a gift exchange, in which each gift must be purchased for a certain dollar amount. Not a spending limit, but a situation where each gift cost the same as the others. This is the perfect example of balanced reciprocity. It is the even exchange of actions, gifts or emotions.

Though this type of reciprocity is not the best way to gain influence with people, balanced or symmetrical reciprocity typically is a psychology that influencers encounter. The emotion that an influencer offers someone can be the same emotion they receive back from that person.

This is why two people, who are very much alike can have completely different opinions about the same individual. It isn't because of who that person is at their core, rather it is the different emotions that person used to interact with the pair. If they were kind to one and impatient with the other, the reactions from the pair will contrast dramatically. It is a form of mirroring, which we will discuss later. It is why trait #3, people with autism rarely judge others, is such an influential trait. If you abstain from judgement of others, then balanced reciprocity says they will not judge you. If you are kind, in turn you will receive kindness. Unfortunately it can work in both positive and negative manners.

In the craze of the "extreme makeovers," televisions shows were making over everything from antique vehicles to people. One of those people was Deleese Williams. She knew her looks were not equivalent to those of her friends or family. It was not that she had an awkward haircut, wore odd clothes or didn't know how to apply makeup. Her differences were structural. From the shape of her eyes to the size of her jawbone, Deleese looked different.

But Deleese had one thing that she could count on. Her family had, by most accounts, always supported her. It was, in a way, her lifeboat in a rough ocean. The support of her family kept her going. But then, the cliched dream of a little girl turned princess became a possibility.

When the producers of the ABC show Extreme Makeover choose Deleese as an episode of their show, most of the family looked past the process of the transformation to the end result. The idea that Deleese would have the opportunity to stand amongst society while not standing out would be a dream come true. But there was a critical part of the process that would have lasting repercussions which no one saw coming.

During the pre-operation consultations and scheduling process, the producers of Extreme Makeover created the ugly duckling segment of the show. This included the background, photos and interview with friends and family of the soon-to-be transformed subject. The producers knew interviews about what a wonderful person the subject was would only go so far. They needed those closest to the future princess to say just how ugly she really was prior to the transformation.

This proved difficult in the case of Deleese. Her family was so supportive and loved her so deeply, that the producers had to coach them into admitting she was ugly. They had spent her entire life supporting Deleese, loving her, and telling her just how beautiful she was.

But eventually family members broke.

Her mother-in-law admitted that, "I never believed my son would marry such an ugly woman." Kelly McGee, Deleese's sister, who had always been a huge source of support, was coached and coerced by the producers to admit difficulties about their childhood because of how Deleese looked. They put words in her mouth to help her describe her ugly sister.

The painful words, even though they were coached and pulled from the family members, hurt Deleese. But this was exactly what the producers wanted. They had Deleese watch as the family said the disparaging things that were leveraged out of them. They wanted to catch the pain Deleese felt when she heard "the truth."

Deleese secretly listened in from an adjacent room as they recorded her hearing just how ugly her family actually thought she was. The producers had successfully captured the hurt and pain they were looking for. But it would all be okay once the process was over. Deleese was hearing about the old version of herself, not the new, elegant, beautiful version that was yet to come.

Deleese was alone in her hotel room in Los Angeles, reading her pre-op instructions when a producer showed up with bad news. The dental surgeon had just informed the show that the recovery time for Deleese would not fit into the shows schedule. It was going to be a much longer wait than they had anticipated and so, as the lawsuit against ABC states, the producer said to Deleese, "You will not be getting an extreme makeover after all…It doesn't fit in our time frame. You will have to go back to Texas tomorrow."

Deleese broke down. She asked, "How can I go back as ugly as I left?"

But, Deleese did go home, exactly as she had left, only crushed. And the hurtful things the producers of the show had coached out of her family could not be unsaid.

The pain of those admissions proved too much for her sister Kelly, and on May 25, 2004 she overdosed, leaving behind two children.

It is hard to over-state the crushing blow that a momentary lapse in judgment had between Deleese and Kelly. Certainly the pain and hurt of the few harsh sentences hung between them in the four months before Kelly's suicide. Kelly, even though she was prodded into hurting Deleese, had hurt her. She had an emotional debt towards her sister that she couldn't pay.

She couldn't unsay what she had been manipulated into saying. She had no way to even the score. Balanced reciprocity, or the even exchange of emotion, explains how decades of kindness between sisters can be washed away by moments of callous, and how decades of callous by a brilliant scientist could wash away his history.

I've heard the golden rule is treat others how you want to be treated, but the platinum rule is treat others how they want to be treated. If this is true, perhaps the manure rule is treat others how they treated you first. This is a version of balanced or symmetrical reciprocity and how history has handled the bitter Robert Hooke.

Remember the quote by Jerry D. Cavin from earlier, "although Hooke was right scientifically...the manner in which Hooke expressed himself in the argument did not win him many friends." Although this was written specifically about his feud with Hevelius, it describes many of Hooke's feuds with fellow scientists, including Isaac Newton.

Many of us were taught the story of Isaac Newton sitting at the bottom of an apple tree, when an apple fell on his head and viola, he "discovered" gravity. Most of us learned this about the same time that we heard the story of George Washington cutting down a cherry tree, but was not able to tell a lie. Or roughly when we heard that most people during the time of Christopher Columbus thought the world was flat, (along with many other myths that grade schools used to fill up lesson plans.) The story, like most of history, is an exaggeration made more palatable for young minds.

Universal gravitation came from the groundbreaking Principia Mathimatica, which Newton published July 5th, 1687. But it did not come as a revelation from an apple falling on his head, as the story goes. There are many references to Newton watching an apple fall, but he was probably more inspired by Christopher Wren, Edmund Halley and Robert Hooke than an apple actually hitting his head. Newtons friend turned biographer, William Stukeley explains the apple story this way.

-After dinner, the weather being warm, we went into the garden and drank tea under the shade of some apple trees, only he and myself. Amidst other discourse he told me he was just in the same situation, as when formerly the notion of gravitation came into his mind. Why should that apple always descend perpendicularly to the ground, though he to himself; occasioned by the fall of an apple as he sat in a contemplative mood. Why should it not go sideways or upwards? But constantly to the earths center. Assuredly, the reason is that the earth draws it. There must be a drawing power in matter and the sum of the drawing power in the matter of the earth must be in the earths center, not in any side of the earth. Therefore does this apple fall perpendicularly, or toward the center. If matter thus draws matter; it must be in proportion of its quantity. Therefore the apple draws the earth as well as the earth draws the apple.-

This is obviously a generality describing the origin, science and math behind universal gravitation. It has many moving parts. One of those parts on which universal gravitation was founded is the law of the inverse square of gravity. This law explains how gravity spreads out to a larger area the further away it is from it's source. But that gravity is also weakened the further it travels. The law of the inverse square is the math by which that area and the strength of the gravity can be calculated depending on it's distance from the source.

Johannes Kepler mentioned that spreading of light from a point source obeys and inverse square law in 1604. Ismael Bullialdus said that "gravity" weakens as the inverse square of the distance it affects in his 1645 book, Astronomia Philolaica. In Micrographia, Robert Hooke touched on how gravity affects the earths atmosphere as it diminishes via the inverse square law.

It was this, and many more confluence of ideas that founded the law of the inverse square of gravity, on which part of universal gravitation was built. And it was this point that Hooke planted another in a string of flags against Newton, arguing that he should have been given credit in Principia Mathematica. He said if it weren't for his work on the law of the inverse square of gravity, universal gravitation would not have come about.

Like much of Hooke's contention he did have a point. Not unlike the groundwork done before a building can be built, many of the people who had touched on the inverse square of gravity helped build the foundation on which Newton erected gravitation. But by the time Principia Mathematica was published, Hooke had positioned himself squarely against Newton, and ensured that balanced reciprocity would work against him in his relationship with Newton.

As early as 1676, Robert Hooke is recorded, in his own letters trying his best to correct Newton about certain scientific equations, that Newton felt were accurate. The details of the letters are excruciating, written in centuries old English which is dry and difficult to decipher. It really has no bearing on our story except to establish that Hooke was difficult to say the least. Most historians feel that Hooke was speculating about

Newton's math, then correcting his own speculations. He seemed to have a knack for inventing a problem where there wasn't one, and then arguing the problem. In a letter to Edmund Halley, Isaac Newton writes this about Hooke.

-Should a man who thinks himself knowing, and loves to show it in correcting and instructing others, come to you, when you are busy, and notwithstanding your excuse press discourse upon you, and through his own mistakes correct you, and multiply discourse; and then make this use of it, to boast that he taught you all he spake, and oblige you to acknowledge it, and cry out injury and injustice if you do not; I believe you would think him a man of strange unsociable temper. Hooke's letters in several respects abounded too much with that humor, which Hevelius and others complain of. . .-

Hooke had already proven himself cantankerous, argumentative and difficult to work with when Principia Mathimatica was published. Newton, right or wrong, was exercising balanced reciprocity when he opted not to credit Hooke for his contribution. If the event were to have occurred in a vacuum, Newton would be unequivocally wrong not to include all contributors to his work. But, that would mean giving credit every mathematician who ever contributed to the study of mathematics. He would have to trace his equations through Copernicus, Archimedes, Pythagoras, Plato and Ptolemy. Obviously Newton couldn't give credit to every mathematician who contributed or the credits would've been longer than the book.

So where to draw the line?

When making the cuts for those whom you admire and wish to give thanks, the man that has plagued you with corrections and discourse is probably an easy cut to make. When asked how much credit Newton gave Hooke for some of his work he said, "Yet am I not beholden to him for any light into that business but only for the diversion he gave me from my other studies to think on these things and for his dogmaticalness in writing as if he had found the motion in the ellipses which inclined me to try it."

After Hooke died, Newton was made the president of the Royal Society. In a widely accepted rumor, it was soon after Newton's ascent that the only painting ever rendered of Robert Hooke disappeared. Some think it was burned, to rid the Royal Society of the black mark the brilliant scientist left.

Today every image of Hooke is nothing more than an artists best guess at what he may have looked like.

This is why, though much of Hooke's work remains, the man has been lost to history. Only two years after Hooke's death, his biographer Richard Waller called him a despicable man, a miserable bastard who jealously guarded ideas he had probably stolen anyway.

The quote, *"If I have seen further than others, it is by standing on the shoulders of giants,"* comes from a letter Newton wrote to Hooke in 1676, during the ebbs and flows of their feud.

It is considered by many an inspirational quote. Some think it is a saying where the author offers a compliment to those who laid the foundations before them, allowing them to do great things. But others, myself included, think it's a double-entendre.

Most of the members of the Royal Society at the time of the writing were of average or above average size. But Hooke suffered from kyphosis, which curved his spine and shortened his stature. When Newton mentioned help from giants, many think he meant to compliment everyone in the Royal Society, but the diminutive Robert Hooke.

If people with autism rarely judge others, Robert Hooke could've taken lesson from them. It seems that Newton, Hevelius, Huygens and many others fell under the judgement of Hooke. Just like Deleese, even if only for a moment, was judged by the comments pulled from her sister by the producers of a fleeting television show.

Once we understand the power of balanced or symmetrical reciprocity, it's easy to see how someone who is not critical of others would hold more influence than those who are.

In the next section we will see how one man spared his judgment, and changed the world with billions of chocolate bars. You'll also learn exactly how an army turned enemy POWs into lifelong supporters.

If there is any doubt about the positive and influential traits of those on the autism spectrum, consider a quote by Professor Michael Fitzgerald who is described this way.

-Michael specializes in Autism, Asbergers syndrome, ADHD and child behavior problems. He has a particular interest in creativity and mental health issues. He has written, co-written, edited and co-edited over 24 book on this specialist subjects and has many peer reviewed publications.-

He said this, "I'm 100% sure that Isaac Newton had Aspergers syndrome," which has been identified as a form of autism.

Up to this point, I have not found anyone who has said the same about Robert Hooke.

Section 2 Kindness, The Power Behind Persuasion

(People with Autism Rarely Judge Others)

Chapter 4
influence achieved

"One is only happy in proportion as he makes others feel happy."
-Milton Hershey

In 2017, Forbes published what they call the Global 2000. These are the 2000 biggest companies in the world according to their ranking system. Hershey was #956 on the list. One of the best illustrations of the influence of Hershey is that, like Apple or Wells Fargo, when you call the company by name, at least in the U.S. everyone knows what it is. When speaking about the company, no one has to say, Hershey, the chocolate company that distributes candy bars world wide.

This recognition does not come from size or money or sales. In fact, the #1 company on the same list is ICBC. Ever heard of it? Perhaps you have, but there are a few ICBC's around. Is it the Insurance Corporation of British Columbia or the Industrial and Commercial Bank of China? Once you hear the full name it becomes apparent which it probably is, but unless you frequent China, or study global economics you most likely did not know, initially.

But you probably do know Hershey. This multi-billion dollar company had almost 18,000 employees in 2017 and $7.44 billion in sales. These numbers put the company at #874 in profit, #533 in market value and #94 in the worlds most valuable brands.

Let me explain that a different way. There are only 93 companies in the world with a more valuable brand than Hershey, which is an astounding feat.

This behemoth success was started on one thing. Not the investments of a community, old money handed down or a new craze that swept the nation. It was initially established on a single belief in the kind man who started it.

Milton Hershey was not a great businessman, when he started.

- In 1876 Hershey failed a printing apprenticeship.
- At 19 Hershey started his first candy business with money from his mother, sister and a man named Harry Lebkicher. It failed.
- He went to Denver to make money in the silver boom, and failed.
- In 1883 he started another candy business in New York, which collapsed.

At this point his mother's side of the family had written him off. They had invested and lost small fortunes on him by this time and his repeated failures were more than most people could handle, except for one man.

One of his first investors, Harry Lebkicher, continued to support Hershey despite the repeated failures. After his failure in New York, Harry paid for Hershey to get his equipment back from the train station that had shipped it, cash on delivery. Hershey was broke. But Lebkicher wasn't, and it was this final investment that launched Hershey into the business stratosphere. With the financial and physical help from Lebkicher he started a successful caramel business that he parlayed into the chocolate empire we all know today.

This is not so much the study of Hershey, but of Lebkicher. Why would a wise, industrious, Civil War survivor continue investing in a proven failure?

Lebkicher was notoriously quiet. It is difficult to find quotes by the man. In fact Hersey himself said, "Lebbie was the only man I couldn't outwork. But I could out talk him. He didn't say much, and when he did, he usually snapped at you."

But one quote attributed to him during his service in the Civil War speaks loudly about the person he was. In reference to his commanding officers he said, "...if the Generals would all work together the war (would have) been at a close, but here the one tries to get more honor than the other to get a fat office."

Lebkicher valued congeniality and working together. Eventually, he was able to find it in the kind and generous Milton Hershey. The examples of Hershey's kindness were amplified after he made his fortune. He was notoriously generous. That kindness and generosity stood out amongst many of the other businessmen of his time.

Hershey operated in the backdrop of atrocities from "businessmen" like Leopold II and Hermann von Siemens.

King Leupold II was heir to the Belgium throne, and in 1865, he took his birthright. Obsessed with building Belgium's overseas footprint, he searched and found an area perfect for European meddling.

It was the Congo.

With its rich natural resources like gold, ivory and rubber, and it's unorganized system of tribes, the Congo was ripe for exploitation. It was exactly the place and people that Leopold felt needed an introduction to Jesus Christ, and in some cases, literally.

Under the guise of spreading Christianity and with borrowed money from the Belgium government for his "humanitarian" project, Leopold forcefully seized control of the Congo partially through a very complicated and underhanded exchange of power with a slave trader named Tippu Tip.

With control over the region, Leopold was able to export it's incredibly profitable natural resources.

After rapidly paying off the debt owed to his homeland, the new enterprise paid Leopold handsomely. But his bloody seizure of the area would pale in comparison to the brutal business practices he employed.

For example, workers who did not meet their daily ivory or gold quota would have a hand or a foot amputated. But if amputating their hands or feet interfered with their work, or if a worker had already missed a quota and couldn't afford to lose another extremity, it was their family that paid the price. Images of men staring at the severed hands and feet of their young children sent a clear message to those who hadn't experienced the brutal practice themselves.

Leopold's agents also "de-populated" areas needed to develop rubber crops. In some instances this meant the eradication of a few sparse dwellings. But in other cases it meant wiping out entire villages. This extermination was not done as a war tactic, but as a means to increase profits.

Hermann von Siemens was another businessman operating during Hershey's life. He ran the manufacturing company that bore his name during WWII. Siemens found a cheap work force in a very unorthodox place; Jewish concentration camps. Siemens amassed a fortune on the backs of the victims of the holocaust.

A very common anecdote attributed to Siemens during this time is, "it was not atypical for a slave worker to build electrical switches for Siemens in the morning and be snuffed out in a Siemens-made gas chamber in the afternoon."

This was the time period in American history that made child labor laws necessary and the gathering of the work force in the form of unions common. Because of the labor-related deaths and mistreatment of workers by business owners during this time, the landscape of the U.S. workforce changed dramatically. A slogan arose during the "Bread and Roses" strike of 1912 in Lawrence Massachusetts that sums up some of the conditions.

"Better to starve fighting than to starve working."

Out of this dark culture, Milton Hershey built an empire by spreading kindness and joy. A description of the book Hershey: Milton S. Hershey's Extraordinary Life of Wealth, Empire and Utopian Dreams says it best. (The author) solidifies his subject's reputation as a kindly type of industrialist. Hershey himself unknowingly explained his own kind nature accidentally in a famous quote attributed to him. He said, "business is a matter of human service."

It was this man in which Harry Lebkicher choose to invest, not Hershey the multi-national conglomerate. It was Milton Hershey, the kind and gentle failure who needed a hand. This honest and gentle spirit, shining in an age of darkness, needed the help of a Civil War vet, and it was that Civil War vet who made the final investment Milton Hershey needed to get his candy making equipment back, and change the world.

But why do people inherently trust and believe in kindness? Is that even true? Perhaps Harry Lebkicher was a crazy old sentimental coot who happened to get lucky. How powerful is kindness when it comes to influence and persuasion?

#3 on the list is, "People with autism rarely judge others." It is perhaps, the personal quality that is driving force behind kindness. If we honestly give everyone a fair shake, regardless of what they have done, will it offer more or less persuasion?

It turns out, kindness and non-judgment are incredibly persuasive, and to understand how, we can look in a very unlikely place. Kindness and reserving judgement was pivotal in Communist prisoner of war camps during the Korean war.

In June of 1957 a young Mike Wallace was broadcast into homes across America. The white smoke drifting up from his cigarette bore a stark contrast to the black background behind him, and the colorless video accentuated the contrast even more.

He opens with, "My guest tonight is the youngest U.S. army turncoat of the Korean War. You see him behind me," a picture of a young, handsome man flashes on the screen next to Wallace.

He continues. "He's David Hawkins of Oklahoma City." The screen goes dark. Suddenly the words, The Mike Wallace Interview flash across the black backdrop with cigarette smoke wafting behind the words as they are simultaneously spoken by a man with a deep voice. For some reason there is the sound of a drum being struck twice. Then the interview starts.

This is the point where the irritation for Wallace becomes visible.

He fidgets with some papers as he explains, "Three years ago the United States was stunned by an announcement from war-torn Korea. U.S. army private David Hawkins and 20 other prisoners of the communists have become turncoats," Wallace over pronounces the word turncoats. He continues, "they had renounced their own country and disappeared behind red China's bamboo curtain." Hawkins is quietly smoking behind him, leaning on the arm of his chair. Wallace partially swivels around, not facing Hawkins but instead, speaking to him from the left side of his face, as if the empty blackness behind Hawkins was more worthy of his attention.

"Dave," Wallace says, "let me ask you this." He goes on to explain that the New York Times had published a piece suggesting the "turncoats" hadn't really converted to communism, but that they had committed crimes against their own, and didn't want to face whatever punishment the U.S. had in store for them.

Hawkins was captured shortly after his 17th birthday. He was shot, lost conciseness, and when he awoke the first words he heard were, "We are friends. We are not going to hurt you." He was being welcomed in a Chinese communist hospital. It was a much warmer welcome than the one he received from Mike Wallace.

The Korean War, like any war, was a complicated political and fundamental contention that, at it's core, pitted capitalism against communism. WWII resulted in the division of Korea along the 38th parallel. The communist controlled, north side butted squarely against the U.S. occupied south. In 1950 the communists from the north crossed the 38th parallel, sparking what would be the Korean War and a debate between communism and capitalism that still rages, in one version or another, today.

As Hawkins awoke to hear the kind words of his doctor, there was no doubt he was uneasy. At the time there were basically two halves of the communist enemy. There was the North Korean half, which often did not recognize the Geneva Convention mandates.

Frequently, South Korean POWs were used as labor for military purposes, which is strictly forbidden by articles 49-57. Or they were indoctrinated to communism, then assigned to the most dangerous battles and positions in the war. The stance of the Koreans in doing this was, why kill ours, when we can kill theirs.

Then there was the Chinese half of the North Korean army. They also frequently ignored the Geneva Convention guidelines, but for a much different reason. They adhered to the Confucian Code. Although Confucianism is a deep system of actions and beliefs, it is often described as being built on three values.

1. Filial Piety. Respect for parents and elders.
2. Ritual. Observance and adherence to systematic signs of respect and faith.
3. Humaneness. Caring and empathy for other humans.

In other words, if you were captured by the North Korean army, you could be captured by a Korean enemy that used you as fodder, or by a Chinese enemy that viewed you as an equal. Hawkins, along with mountains of others, was captured by the Chinese.

So many soldiers were captured that the Chinese army had to hire hundreds of staff to manage the POW camps. Amongst those hired was Zhou Shangun, a translator. She said of the POWs, "They didn't know our policy. They didn't know if we were going to kill them, or force them to do hard labor or keep them in China forever and not let them return home. So they worried a lot."

But most, at that point had little to worry about. Qian Meide, who was also a translator said, "My supervisor asked me to read the regulations to the POWs. It began with 'Dear Students.' I was very surprised and asked why, because to me they were prisoners and we were their captors. My supervisor said yes, they are students and you are instructors."

The Chinese often held lectures and classes for the prisoners, athletic events between camps and essay contests for the POWs. It was the latter that produced the comments of U.S. soldiers, which the Chinese used as propaganda.

After the soldier experienced unexpectedly kind treatment, great meals, and lectures explaining the communist view of the world, the Chinese captors would offer small prizes to the winners of essay contests. More often than not, the winners of these prizes had dotted their essays with small, pro-communists statements. After all, these men had come to Korea with the purpose of killing the Chinese. Now, those same Chinese were treating them better than some had ever been treated at home. William White, a black POW said of the Chinese, "For the first time in my life, I have witnessed complete equality."

In his fabulous book, Influence, The Psychology of Persuasion, Robert Cialdini explains why the Chinese offered small prizes for men who won these contests. He explains that, not only were the little, pro-communist statements great for propaganda, but they also held a deeper, psychological power.

The power of written commitment.

The prizes for these essay contest were kept purposefully small. Cialdini explains that items such as small bags of rice went to the winners. The reason was the Chinese wanted their POWs to own what they had written. They needed the authors to think they themselves believed the small incremental shifts that were happening in their opinions.

If a prisoner was offered something very valuable for his winning essay, he could explain away his writings. But no one would compromise their beliefs for a bag of rice, would they?

The answer is not simply yes or no. It depends on the value they placed on the rice. They would not place massive value on a bag of rice, if they were being treated as guests rather than prisoners. Imagine the poor souls detained in the Korean POW camps. If they were offered the opportunity to build a bridge rather than fight their own, on the front lines, in the most dangerous places, for the enemy, just for writing a pro-communist essay, it would be easy to explain away writing almost anything.

But what is a bag of rice to a man who is so healthy, he is competing in athletic events? The reason a bag of rice was a small prize had everything to do with the condition of the recipient.

In an article by Reuters named, American POWs remember life in Japanese prison camps, Wayne Miller explained that their food ration was usually two bowls of rice, with little meat or vegetables. Imagine offering that prisoner a bag of rice for a sentence degrading capitalism. That bag of rice could double his calories for a day. When you are starving, that is a huge reward. But, the men under the kinder, Chinese control in Korea weren't starving. So the bag of rice seemed small, and the sentence written supporting communism seemed their own.

Not long after the contentious beginning of the Mike Wallace interview with David Hawkins, Wallace is finally facing Hawkins. He asks, "You became a turncoat…Why? What did you have against the United States?"

Hawkins voice is soft and quiet. He answers, "Well Mike it wasn't actually that I had, uh, something against the United States." He stops. Perhaps the longest pause during the interview. Hawkins seems to be searching for his own, actual feelings. He goes on, "I underwent the, uh, mass indoctrination program that the Chinese, uh, instigated in the camp, and there was a lot of things that they told me that, uh, sounded to me like common sense."

As part of the agreement of peace, a 90-day window was offered to any soldier to consider, or reconsider his choice. If they had initially renounced their citizenship, they could change their mind and choose a repatriation plan. After denouncing the U.S. two soldiers did change their mind. Edward Dikenson and Claude Batchelor returned home. They were both immediately court-martialed. Their repatriation plan included prison sentences. Batchelor served four and a half years and Dikenson three and a half, but both were sentenced to much more.

Lewis Griggs, one of the "turncoats" said in a televised interview, "Even if I had wanted repatriation, the fate of Dikenson and Batchelor would stop me."

The judgement passed by the U.S. and the Senator from Wisconsin, Joe McCarthy proved more than some could handle. Even today the word McCarthyism symbolizes reckless and unsubstantiated accusations and judgment, which is the opposite of #3 on the list; "People with autism rarely judge others."

It is also the opposite of how a foreign car manufacturer completely turned around the worst assembly plant in the United States 30 years later.

In 1982 General Motors was forced to shut down the Fremont California plant. It was widely accepted that Fremont was the worst auto factory in the world. Commenting on the employees at Fremont, Bruce Lee (not the martial artist but the manger for the western region for United Auto) said, "It was considered the worst workforce in the automobile industry in the United States."

But, on Dec. 10th, 1984, Toyota renamed the plant New United Motor Manufacturing Inc. or NUMMI, and began making Chevy Novas. Many were skeptical about the success of the new plant. Most of that skepticism came from part of the agreement GM had made with UAW.

The part in question was that NUMMI had to hire 80% of laid off employees from the original plant. These were the same people who were, "the worst workforce in the automobile industry."

Rumors of on the job antics including prostitutions, drinking, drug use and purposeful sabotage of the vehicles at the Fremont plant were admitted by many of those who performed the acts themselves. Prior to the 1982 shut down, the plant resembled more of a brothel/bar combination than a workplace.

But, GM had one rule that was always obeyed. That rule was, the line doesn't stop. As a chassis rolled into workers areas on the never stopping line, workers had to assemble it as it went. Henry Ford pioneered the assembly line and GM wasn't about to stop the process that had been working for almost a century.

The rumor was that it costs $15,000/minute to stop the line. So the culture of Fremont was one of, drinking on the job, prostitution in the parking lot, drug use during work, but never, ever stop the line. If an employee had a problem installing their given piece of the car, that employee would mark the car and let it continue down the line. Often the repair would not be made until the car was fully assembled.

This was the mindset and culture of the workers Toyota had agreed to re-hire. The question on everyones mind was how could they turn this around? The answer was with kindness. Kindness in the form of a fixture in Toyota plants called andon chords, and a completely different management style.

In the book Smarter, Faster, Better, Charles Duhigg tells the story of Rick Madrid, an employee of Fremont and NUMMI who travelled to Japan to see what Toyota manufacturing looked like. He watched a worker struggle with a bolt. Rather than continue, the worker pulled an andon cord. The entire line stopped at the end of the station. As it did, the man's direct leaders took orders from him, handing him tools and assisting him with the bolt. Once the bolt was fixed the man pulled the cord and work resumed.

Madrid said of the event, "I just couldn't believe it. Back home I had watched a guy fall in the pit, and they didn't stop the line." In Jan 1985, a month after opening the plant, Tetsuro Toyota, the newly appointed president of the plant, was observing the assembly lines. Duhigg explains that Toyota watched an employee struggle with a particular tail light installation. As the man struggled Toyota approached him, read the name on his uniform and said, "Joe, please pull the cord."

"I can fix this sir," Joe said. Toyota repeated himself, "Joe, please pull the cord." Eventually Toyota guided Joe's hand to the andon cord and they pulled it together, stopping the line.

Joe, overcoming his fear, fixed the tail light. Toyota bowed to Joe afterwards and said, "Joe, please forgive me. I have done a poor job of instructing your managers of the importance of helping you pull the cord when there is a problem. You are the most important part of this plant. Only you can make every car great. I promise I will do everything in my power to never fail you again."

This simple cord and kind gesture from Toyota instantly put the management and the workers at NUMMI on the same side rather than at each others throats. By 1986 their productivity was higher than any other GM plant and double what it had done when it was GM Fremont. It happened with essentially the same work force and in about one year. The main difference was that workers were not judged for stopping the line, and management was kind enough to help.

History has painted a picture of Robert Hooke as unkind, judgmental and not very influential in the absence of an actual painting of the man. But Milton Hershey was the opposite. He personified kindness. One story tells that, during the Great Depression, Milton Hershey was deeply involved in the building of his town, Hershey Pennsylvania. Times were tough and work was slow. So, rather than lay people off, he sent workers from the chocolate factory to work on town projects. At one point he had the opportunity to buy a steam shovel that could, as the story goes, "do the work of 40 men." Milton Hershey apparently said, "Get rid of the steam shovel, and bring back the 40 men!"

In section 3 we will jump from the depression era to the digital revolution, and from a kindly gentleman to psychopaths.

Many people believe that Hershey, the company, was built on the kindness of Milton Hershey, which certainly is very true. But it started with the kindness of a little known man named Harry Lebkicher.

Lebbie was kind enough to help a friend over and over, and never pass judgement on his failures. It was a trait he instinctively understood was valuable. It was something the Chinese communists knew was persuasive. It was a value that Japanese auto manufactures relied upon to build an incredible workforce. If it is true that people with autism rarely judge others, history has repeatedly proven that to be a massively influential quality.

At Lebbie's funeral, Milton Hershey said, "We've just buried the best friend I've ever had."

Section 3 Oxytocin and Psychopaths

(People With Autism Are Not Tied to Social Expectations)

Chapter 5
influence failed

"This scandal was brought to you by the digital revolution."
- Monica Lewinsky

Justine had no idea that her entire life was about to explode.

She was the pretty, influential director of corporate communications at IAC. Today IAC is traded on the NASDAQ. They are an internet and media company built of brands such as Investopia, Vimeo, OK Cupid, Angie's List, Tinder and Match.com to name just a few. But our story is not set today. Our story starts ten days before 2014.

Justine had just landed in Cape Town South Africa. As she completed the 11 hour flight from New York she turned on her phone.

That was the beginning of the end.

A text from someone she hadn't spoken to in over a decade captured her attention. "I'm so sorry to see what's happening," came the surprising sentence.

During her flight the hashtag #HasJustineLandedYet was trending worldwide.

In reverse chronology she began to see tweets such as, "We are about to watch this @JustineSaaco bitch get fired. In REAL time. Before she even KNOWS she's getting fired."

There was the comment from her employer, IAC, which read, "This is an outrageous, offensive comment. Employee in question currently unreachable on an intl flight."

One read, "I'm an IAC employee and I don't want @JustineSaaco doing any communications on our behalf ever again. Ever."

Every one of those tweets came true. Justine was driven into hiding by hate speech and threats to her life. Even at the time of this writing, she is somewhat of a social media recluse.

Justine made a critical error in the last tweet she sent out before the flight.

She made a joke.

But, there was a problem with the joke. It was incredibly sarcastic. In her attempt to shine light on the pristine bubble of white America, Justine combined race, politics and disease in one joke, on a medium where sarcasm doesn't always translate.

She wrote, "Going to Africa. Hope I don't get AIDS. Just kidding. I'm white!"

It was her, albeit insensitive, way of saying, "Now that the AIDS epidemic is under control for rich, white America, no one cares about it anymore."

Or possibly, "Because of the fortunate, white bubble of safety around me, I don't have to worry about AIDS."

Unfortunately the Twitterverse did not take it that way. It was taken literally by a few influential people, then piled on by their audience to the tune of tens of thousands of hateful, name calling, threatening tweets in response.

Justine's life was completely altered during that 11 hour flight and she had no idea. She had unknowingly hitched her social wagon to one misunderstood sentence.

But why in the world would the director of corporate communications, or for that matter anyone, allow themselves to offer up such an easily misunderstood sentence? Why, in her attempt to be funny, was she blind to the manner in which that sentiment could be construed? How could she give up her influence for one stupid attempt at humor?

The answer is that she, like a lot of us, was an addict.

Drug addicts often describe the feeling of euphoria as beginning the moment they decide to get high, not when they do the drug. Or as soon as they obtain their drug or choice the high starts, rather than when the chemicals enter their body. Not only do they feel the effects before they use, but they get addicted to the process as well. The lifestyle, money and paraphernalia are as much a part of the addiction as the drug itself.

Consider this sentiment, written by a former drug dealer under a pseudonym on substance.com about the addictive aspects of the lifestyle of dealing drugs.

-When people discuss drug addiction, treatment and recovery, they tend to spare little sympathy for the dealers. They're the ones causing the problem, right? But a high proportion of dealers are addicted themselves—and not just to drugs.

I started dealing shortly after I began using—initially to support my own habit. I was smoking weed and hash at the age of 13 and by the time I was 17, I was supplying marijuana and LSD to 15 colleges in five states on the East Coast. I was definitely addicted to substances: I smoked, drank alcohol or tripped on acid daily. But I was also addicted to the money, to the lifestyle I was living and to the status they earned me.

I craved the outlaw image. When I walked into a party it was like I was a celebrity, with the girls whispering my name and wanting to meet me. Everyone gave me the ultimate respect because I was the connect, the dude that was holding.

I craved the superficial freedom that selling drugs granted me—the ability to do what I wanted and go where I wanted, whenever I wanted. I went to Hawaii once. I just said, "Let's go" and paid cash for four round-trip tickets. The ticket lady looked at me like, "You're paying cash? Are you serious?" I took three buddies and we stayed in Honolulu, then hopped over to Hilo and rented a house. We stayed for two months, partying, chasing girls, surfing, spear fishing and jumping off cliffs, and I paid for everything.

I was living a dream, reveling in my ability to bring my peers exotic brands of marijuana and LSD, so that they could enjoy new experiences. I was a connoisseur of high-quality merchandise, of kind bud and excellent trips.

It all ended with a drug arrest at age 20, resulting in a 25-year mandatory minimum federal drug sentence for a first-time, nonviolent offense. A harsh reality for a kid barely out of his teens, and a sobering one.

That was in 1993. I'm still in federal prison today. During my time inside, I eventually not only quit using all drugs but also had to address my craving for the dealing lifestyle. I'm convinced that both were equally addictive. And I'm not the only one—the existence of a fellowship like Hustlers Anonymous testifies to that. So do dozens of the men who have done time with me over the last 20 years, often small-time dealers who were hooked on the process and lifestyle of selling drugs.

"I'm in prison for selling crack," says Ben, a 24-year-old African American from St. Louis who is doing a five-year sentence. "I used to smoke a little bud and drink some forties, but I didn't really get ****** up. I was about my money. I was on a paper chase, for real. If I was addicted to anything, it was getting money."

Ben, who grew up in a rough area of South City in St. Louis, didn't feel like he had many other employment options. "Everybody in the hood is involved in drugs in some way," he tells me. "My mom was a crackhead and my dad was in prison my whole life. I was just doing what's natural. In my hood if you're about anything, then you're getting money."

"I wish I didn't get high at all," he continues, "because that's how I got caught slipping. When I go back out there I'm gonna be drug-free. That's how it's gotta be if you want to make money. I'm still sick behind this stuff—I need my fix."

If one definition of addiction is compulsively continuing to do something, despite negative consequences, young men like Ben fit the mold perfectly. Why else would they plan to take the crazy risk of getting busted again for something that they've already done time for?

Black has a similar story. Born and bred in New York City, this 35-year-old Puerto Rican is doing a 15-year stretch for selling cocaine and carrying a firearm. "My thought process has always been, 'If I have a gun, I can get money,'" Black tells me. "I grew up in the South Bronx, where you had to stay strapped. For real I don't even do drugs—I just drink Cristal. I like the finer things in life: money, BMWs, Rolexes, Armani and gorgeous women. That's why I sold drugs—to get the things I couldn't afford. You see it in rap videos, in the magazines, in the movies, and you want it. I'm addicted to money, power and respect, just like Biggie said."

Our understanding of addiction is evolving to accept that it can apply not only to drugs, but to behaviors like compulsive internet use, eating and sex. Numerous studies suggest that the "high" of certain behaviors may affect our brains in similar ways to drugs. DSM-5, the updated version of the American Psychiatric Association's diagnostic manual published last year, included a new category on behavioral addictions. "Gambling disorder" is the only one currently listed as a diagnosable condition, but "Internet gaming disorder" is mentioned as meriting further research. Logic suggests that new studies will bring other conditions into future editions. From where I'm standing, selling drugs should be under consideration, too.

As a teenager I was living in the middle-class suburbs of affluent Fairfax, Virginia, so unlike Ben, I had other options to make enough money to get high. It's not always the kid from the bad side of the tracks that first seeks to emulate the Scarface lifestyle, then finds he can't let go of it—just like the junkie who keeps sticking the needle in his arm, even when he can't find a vein.

Of course, for many dealers, their addiction to the drug itself does remain primary. "I sold LSD, mushrooms, weed, whatever I could to support my heroin habit," says Aaron, a white 44-year-old Massachusetts native and former "Deadhead" who is doing a 17-year sentence for an LSD conspiracy charge. "I wasn't even a big drug dealer. Everything I made off hooking dudes up went toward heroin and staying on tour. I followed the Dead, then Phish and finally Bonnaroo, Burning Man and other festivals."

"I would move lots of acid on the lot and do mail order to dudes all over the country," Aaron says. "I would basically sell anything I could get a hold of. But everything was geared toward getting that next hit."

I used to love the rituals, love getting loads of weed and breaking it up into one-pound Ziploc bags. I used to love counting the money. The whole process.

I saw myself as a high-level businessman. But the truth is, it's a miracle I was even able to run my drug business while smoking weed and drinking all day. I would make my rounds, drop off drugs, pick up money, fly to different states to arrange shipments and coordinate their arrival. I thought this represented total freedom, but I was a slave to that lifestyle.

Christopher Hoss is a pseudonym for a writer who is in a federal prison, serving 25 years for drug trafficking.-

How is it possible that the dealer becomes more addicted to the lifestyle than some of their clients are to the drug itself?

The answer is that some of the addictive chemicals have already been released by their own brain without using the drug. In fact, in some cases people are more addicted to the chemicals released by their brain than by a chemical artificially inserted in their bodies. The National Institute on Drug Abuse explains the science behind addiction in their article Drugs, Brains, and Behavior: The Science of Addiction incredibly well. This excerpt explains what happens to the the brain of the addict.

-Most drugs of abuse directly or indirectly target the brain's reward system by flooding the circuit with dopamine. Dopamine is a neurotransmitter present in regions of the brain that regulate movement, emotion, motivation, and feelings of pleasure. When activated at normal levels, this system rewards our natural behaviors. Overstimulating the system with drugs, however, produces euphoric effects, which strongly reinforce the behavior of drug use—teaching the user to repeat it.-

Another way to reference this addiction is to think of adrenaline junkies. They are driven to put themselves in incredibly dangerous situations, not to save a life, help humanity or even to make money. They are addicted to the "natural" high created in their body by the release of different chemicals in their own bodies, including dopamine, and it's done completely without the use of drugs.

It was almost the same addiction Justine faced when she posted her absent-minded tweet.

During a positive social interaction the chemical oxytocin is released into our blood. Positive social interactions can include getting the phone number of someone to whom you are attracted, getting help from a trusted friend or telling a joke that makes people laugh.

Paul J. Zak, the professor at Claremont Graduate University who popularized "neuroeconomics," an emerging field that combines economics with biology, neuroscience, and psychology and perhaps the leading authority on oxytocin says, "Conversation rich in social content builds trust, which has the effect of a verbal massage or oral grooming and releases oxytocin."

But what does oxytocin have to do with addiction?

Oxytocin is deeply linked to trust and social interaction, but it doesn't work alone. A study from the National Center of Biotechnology Information was published called Oxytocin, Motivation and the Role of Dopamine. In it the interaction between oxytocin and dopamine is very convincingly laid out. The following is an excerpt from he study.

-oxytocin and dopamine do not act alone but rather appear to interact with one another to regulate the formation of pair bonds. For instance, it appears that both D2 receptors and oxytocin receptors must be stimulated in order to facilitate the formation of partner preferences (Liu and Wang, 2003). Injection of a D2-receptor antagonist into the nucleus accumbens of female prairie voles can prevent partner preference formation induced by oxytocin and oxytocin antagonists can block partner preference formation induced by D2-receptor agonist administration. In sum, these data suggest that both oxytocin and dopamine work together to influence partner preference formation-

When Justine made the stupid joke on Twitter it wasn't a brutal racist opinion from a cold and uncaring person. It was an attempt for one more hit, one more high for a dopamine/oxytocin addict. "Christopher Hoss" was as addicted to the process of selling drugs as his clients were to the drugs themselves because of the stimulus it triggered in his own brain. That dopamine/oxytocin bath his brain felt is very close to the same high Justine felt when her social status was elevated on Twitter with a funny joke. Unfortunately that high drove them both to ruin.

It can drive otherwise intelligent and caring people to do harmful and hurtful things. The addiction to this social high can cause bright and caring people to act in ways they would never dream of, if it weren't for the impairment caused by oxytocin and it's partner dopamine.

The audience is silent as the speaker begins.

"At the age of 22 I fell in love with my boss, and at the age of 24 I learned the devastating consequences."

At this point the speaker asks for a show of hands from people in the audience who have never made a mistake at the age of 22.

No one moves a muscle.

The social high and flattery of being seduced by someone above you on the hierarchal chain is a perfect recipe for a flood of oxytocin. The trust and compassion this person can trigger depends on just how charming they are and how much authority they have over you.

Most of us who have been affected by the chemical rush of oxytocin have made poor decisions in the social setting that triggered the flood. We know how easy it is for others to say they would never do something when they have never been tempted. Boundaries and limits can be situational. Partially because the chemical rush we feel in the moment can be stronger than our convictions.

When a young woman falls prey to her powerful and charismatic boss, they will often look back and wonder why they made that choice. They have no idea their choices were being affected by an incredibly powerful chemical cocktail happening in their own mind. The fallout from the relationship seems obvious with the benefit of hindsight, but the social setting and the euphoric feeling can be overwhelming in the moment. Especially when your boss is the most powerful man in the free world, and you are his intern.

When Monica Lewinsky spoke the quote above at her TED talk in 2014 she had been virtually silent for decades because of the shame she felt over her choice to interact in the affair.

Her influence was crushed.

While her "boss" traveled around the world with the protection of the United States government, demanding hundreds of thousands of dollars to speak to loving and caring crowds, Lewinsky disappeared into the pit of depression and suicidal thoughts.

The constant fallout from her scandal dwarfed what Justine Saaco experienced. It was the first national and international scandal covered and pined over almost non-stop by political commentators, news media and digital shamers. It was the seed of what is now the cyberbullying forest.

Her influence was crushed by just a few choices she made as a young 22 year-old, heavily impaired by the chemicals in her own brain. Of course she isn't completely innocent in all this. In her talk she admits that she made multiple mistakes. We all have free agency and can choose the situations in which we participate. But when we make choices that seem senseless at the time, it helps to understand the chemicals involved.

Oytocin and dopamine are not criminals. They are very crucial molecules to the development of ourselves and society. But, as with most things, there is a balance between what is healthy and what is not. When that balance is tipped to the extreme it can drive us to make poor choices, say things that aren't true and ruin our influence. These molecules are a huge driving force for all of us, except a limited few.

The most prevalent disorder in which the processing of oxytocin is limited is autism. Those on the spectrum have been shown to have either a limited amount of oxytocin in their blood and spinal fluid or a limited number of oxytocin receptors in their brains that aid in the processing of oxytocin.

It can cause them to be honest when society asks for discretion. It could be why Basil offered a steak to Ivan in public during lent. The need for the oxytocin high associated with positive social interaction has never developed in those on the spectrum. They don't care if you agree, smile when they talk or laugh at their jokes.

It causes extreme truthfulness.

But perhaps that truthfulness is what gave Basil the influence to speak into Ivan's life. When a witness takes the stand in the United States they are asked to "tell the truth, the whole truth and nothing but the truth." We hold the truth in extremely high regard and when we feel someone is being honest we tend to listen. Which makes them more influential, if we allow them a place in society, like Basil had.

The socially disconnected element to autism can be linked directly to the inability to process oxytocin. It is not the cause of autism. Many people think that autism is defined by the persons inability to connect socially and that isn't true. It is simply a side effect of the disease that is very apparent.

But it is a side effect that can cause them to be extremely influential to those around them.

There is another group of people who suffer from a lack of oxytocin processing abilities, causing difficulties with social norms. Unlike Monica Lewinsky and Justine Saaco, this group is immune to social expectations like those on the spectrum. That immunity, though it causes many problems, also leads to them being incredibly influential and persuasive, even more so than those on the spectrum.

Much like those on the autism spectrum, they are not hampered by the social necessities of living up to the expectations of others. Unfortunately they also are incredibly manipulative and selfish.

Though our blunt friends on the spectrum may be very honest, the other group is not. They have no social connection but are able to manipulate social situations to get what they want. This lack of social connection, though a powerful tool for them, can be an absolute affliction to the people with whom they are associated.

Those people are called psychopaths.

James Fallon is a neurobiologist at UC Irvine, Fallon made a name for himself decoding the psychopathic brain. He made waves when, during one of his studies he noticed a brain scan from someone in his own family that proved they were a psychopath.

The person in his family who had the unfortunate scan was himself.

We will dig more into the curious case of Dr. Fallon later, but as perhaps the foremost expert on psychopathy because of his education and first hand experience, Fallon gives us a fascinating list of what he says are the most psychopathic U.S. presidents ever.

Number one is Teddy Roosevelt, according to Fallon. FDR, JFK, and Bill Clinton also top the list.

Section 3 Oxytocin and Psychopaths

(People With Autism Are Not Tied to Social Expectations)

Chapter 6
influence achieved

"I didn't know what made people want to be friends. I didn't know what made people attractive to one another. I didn't know what underlay social interactions." -Ted Bundy

Would you admit to a crime you didn't commit?

What if you thought you were guilty?

In 1985, Helen Wilson was brutally raped and murdered in Beatrice Nebraska. In 1989 Ada JoAnn Taylor confessed to the murder. Today she says that sometimes she can still feel the fabric from the throw pillow in her hands as she suffocated the life out of the sixty-eight year old grandmother.

In 1985, Taylor's life was anything but average. She was the product of years of physical abuse, a failed foster care system, drug and alcohol addictions and was diagnosed by Dr. Wayne Price with borderline personality disorder. She had given up her parental rights to the daughter she birthed at a very young age at the request of Dr. Price. But with the help of a young, gay, pornographic film star named Joseph White, she was attempting to get her rights back.

It was during this tumultuous time in Taylors life that a hog farmer named Burdette Searcey made a promise to the daughter of Helen Wilson. He promised to solve her mother's murder. As a former officer of the Beatrice Police Department, Burdette felt the need to be involved and perhaps needed a reason to get off of the pig farm.

In two short years, Searcey was deputized in Gage County and took on the case full time.

The department and the pig farmer were working from two perspectives.

1. Because of the details of the rape, the authorities at the time decided the murderer was a homosexual.
2. They also determined, from sample taken at the scene, the culprit had type B blood.

In March of 1989 Secrecy had an arrest warrant issued for Taylor and her gay friend Joseph White. The warrant was issued on the basis that White was a homosexual. Also, they had the testimony of a seventeen year old whom the Beatrice Police Department described as "a maybe retard," who said the friends had talked about committing the murder.

White was arrested and during his interrogation he said the idea that he had committed a murder was, "pure, deep bull****." The next day Taylor was arrested. During her interview she explained that she, "blocks a lot of bad things out," and that, "there's a lot in my childhood I can't remember."

It was at this point that her old counselor, Dr. Wayne Price was brought in. He explained to the duo that their recollection of the murder might come to them segmented, a piece here and a piece there. Or that it might occur in dreams.

This shift in the conversation was subtle and is a common, psychological trick the doctor used to turn the conversation from "did you do it" to "how did you do it." Taylor said, "In my head and in my heart, I know I wasn't there." But that didn't persuade Dr. Price or Searecy.

Finally Taylor broke. She admitted to the murder. But there were flaws in her admission. For example, she explained how the event happened in a house. Her description of the house resembled one where she had been abused as a child. Only after it was revealed to her that the murder had taken place in an apartment did she "remember" it that way.

Unfortunately for Searcey neither Taylor nor White had type B blood. After some prodding, Taylor admitted that she thought her childhood friend, Tom Winslow may have been involved. He was also believed to be homosexual and, after his arrest, a bout of questioning and some unconventional memory recollection, admitted he may have been involved.

But Winslow had the wrong blood type as well.

Helen Wilsons niece, Debra Sheldon was brought in for questioning. She was acquainted with Taylor and White during the time of the murder and after unconventional interrogations admitted that she also may have played a role in the murder.

Her blood wasn't type B either.

And so the the slippery slope was slid, with one person being coached into a confession. Then the evidence wouldn't line up. So the confessor points to another possible culprit, and the pattern was repeated until, all told, 6 people were implicated in the murder and rape of Helen Wilson. They were Ada JoAnn Taylor, Thomas Winslow, Joseph White, Kathy Gonzalez, James Dean and Debra Shelden. 5 of the six admitting to their involvement. Only White proclaimed his innocence throughout the ordeal.

The group was called the Beatrice six and were sentenced to decades in prison. Joseph White was the only one to go to trial, as he was the only one that wouldn't confess. So three of the other five testified against him as part of a plea bargain to reduce their sentences.

James Dean admitted that he was present during the rape and murder. He offered testimony that was very descriptive of the event. He said White and Winslow committed the rape. He said that Taylor held a pillow over the face of Wilson which ultimately lead to her death.

Shelden admitted that she was there, but tried to intervene. In her description, White struck her and she didn't remember much after that point. Almost all of the descriptions came from very unconventional tactics. James Dean said in a 1989 deposition, 70-90% of his recollection coming from dreams.

The jury that convicted the group was not informed that the fingerprints from the scene did not match any of the alleged participants in the crime or the victim Helen Wilson.

The jury also never learned that the DNA samples taken from the crime scene were possible matches for Gonzales and Winslow, but that one man, who was a perfect match, had been ruled out by Joyce Gilchrist.

Gilchrist was nicknamed "Black Magic" for her ability to make DNA connections that other forensic examiners couldn't. She was able to make those connections because they were repeatedly wrong. Michael Blair was sentenced to death for murder based on Gilchrist's testimony that his hair matched hair found at the scene.

This turned out to be false.

Curtis McCarty spent 20 years on death row after Gilchrist mishandled his evidence. He was released in 2007 but has not received any compensation. Jeffery Pierce was convicted of rape based on Gilchrist's evidence despite having an airtight alibi. Peirce was released in 2001 after 15 years in prison when the DNA evidence was re-examined and found to be inaccurate.

Gilchrist's testimony or evidence led to the execution of 11 people. But in this case, she ruled out a man named Bruce Allan Smith, a name that would become extremely important.

Ultimately White, who proclaimed his innocence entirely, was convicted and sentenced to life in prison. Winslow plead no contest as part of a plea bargain and received 50 years in prison. Gonzalez, Dean and Shelden all received 10 year sentences and Taylor received 10-40 years after each plead guilty to their part in the crime.

Gonzales, Sheldon and Dean were released after four and a half years. White and Winslow appealed over and over. They were repeatedly denied until 2007. During that appeal DNA testing proved the murderer to be Bruce Allan Smith, who had been dead for 15 years at the time of the appeal.

Joseph White had been right all along. The Beatrice Six had absolutely no involvement.

Gage County eventually was ordered to pay $28 million to the Beatrice six who had almost unanimously admitted to the crime. The group collectively spent over 70 years imprisoned for a crime in which they had no involvement, but admitted to committing.

How is it that not just one, but multiple people remember, admit to and serve prison sentences for committing a murder that none of them had committed?

In 1931 a psychologist named Norman Maier may have found the answer during a very simple experiment.

Maier was interested in understanding how people solve problems. He devised a puzzle which has since become known as the "two cord puzzle".

He hung two cords from the ceiling of his lab. The cords were far enough apart that people could not grab each at the same time. Then he asked people to come up with ways to tie the two ends of the cords together.

Most participants came up with solutions that involved using the items in the lab to reach one cord while holding the other. Extension cords were tied to the end of the ropes, poles were used to hook the end and pull the two cords together and other miscellaneous solutions were created. But Maier had another solution in mind. He wanted to see how long in took people to come up with his solution. So he continued asking the participants to come up with new ways to solve the puzzle, until they ran out of ideas.

The solution Maier was looking for was to swing one rope in a pendulum fashion. Then participants could grab the other rope and catch the swinging rope when it came towards them. Very few participants worked out this solution, until they were given a seemingly accidental clue.

During the experiment, Maier would walk around the lab until, when people had run out of ideas, he would brush against one of the ropes and set it swinging motion. Most people, after seeing the swinging rope, would arrive at Maiers solution.

This experiment showed how easily we can be nudged with a solution to a problem without realizing it. But that wasn't the interesting part.

The fascinating part came after the experiment ended.

When the participants in Maier's experiment were asked, only one-third of them realized they'd been given a clue when Maier bumped the rope. The other two-thirds explained that they arrived at the solution themselves. They fully believed they had solved the puzzle, without help, even though their own thinking did not instigate the solution to the problem.

The majority of participants were easily persuaded to solve the puzzle Maiers way, with Maiers help, the whole time thinking it was their idea.

It happened through a psychological concept called priming.

Imagine this. I show you pictures of delicious food for 30 seconds. Then blindfold you and expose you to the smells of those same great dishes. Then I quickly remove the blindfold and in front of you is a whiteboard with the letters S-O-_-P. I ask you to fill in the missing letter. Instinctively you will most likely spell the word soup. In fact you probably thought that was the answer before I explained it.

But, with a little priming I can change the answer.

Imagine now that I showed you images of dishes being cleaned, brooms and clean laundry. Then I blindfold you and expose you to the smell of lemony cleaners and bleach and pull off your blindfold to the same puzzle.

S-O-_-P now becomes soap.

Priming is another example of a heuristic, like loss aversion from the introduction of this book. The context and situations we are in affects our thinking, decision making and even memory.

Remember, heuristics are shortcuts or rules of thumb that our brain uses to speed up our decision making process. They are, for the most part a good thing. But they can be very easily manipulated.

Here is another example of the priming heuristic.

Ray is an eighth grader who wants to play a joke on his little brother Tom. He tells Tom to spell the word white, which Tom does. Then he asks what color paper plates are. Tom says they are white. So far he's two for two. Ray then tells Tom to spell the color of snow, which of course is w-h-i-t-e.

Finally Ray tells Tom to spell what cows drink as fast as possible. Tom thinks he's being tricked into spelling white again and smugly spells m-i-l-k. Ray laughs and explains to his very primed little brother that cows drink w-a-t-e-r.

I have even used priming in this book. Consider the chapter on Hindenburg from earlier. I wanted you to link Hindenburg the man with the Hindenburg the exploding blimp tragedy. So when describing how his name went down in history I wrote the following.

-Hindenburg had a ***burning*** dislike for Communism, which drove many of his actions. He was chosen to lead his people often in battle and politics, and his name has gone down in history. His actions ***sparked*** a famous, worldwide event and qualified him for the second chapter of this book, but probably not for the reason you think.-

(I hope we are still friends)

Priming is a very powerful, psychological tool that manipulators can use to influence their victims into thinking that poor choices were their idea. They corrupt the mind of the innocent with thoughts that lead to the actions they are trying to illicit.

In a junior high school joke it can be funny.

In a book it can bring out the feelings or memories the author wants.

But when lives, prison or even money is on the line it is purely manipulation.

Ada JoAnn Taylor's hair is streaked with grey through the natural looking jet black tones, and cut short during her interview. She looks haggard and exhausted. It seems like she has spent years missing sleep. During the three minute interview there is one moment when she appears to twist her face into the closest representation of a smile that she can seem to muster. It happens when she uncovers a ridiculous truth about the investigation. Price, her one time mental therapist, was also a part-time sheriff's deputy who aided in the interrogations.

The same man whom she had trusted to give her advice about her mental health years earlier was now interrogating her. "We know you did this," she quoted Price, "we know you suffocated her. If you'll just concentrate on your dreams your memories will come back. You've just repressed your memories."

The cord has been set in motion.

The interviewer then says, "but the suggestion that you may have done it was enough to get you to admit," and right on cue, Ada JoAnn Taylor begins repeating, verbatim what the interviewer is saying, immediately after she says it. It is almost as if the interviewer is now doing the priming.

Taylor says of Price, who helped wrongly convict 6 people of murder, that being privy to her background and psychological state, he knew, "if we tell her something hard enough she's going to listen to it. She's gonna accept it."

She says the Searecy would tell her the police knew she had suffocated Wilson with a pillow. It is the tormenting false memory that still runs rampant in Taylors mind. She says she can still visualize herself holding the couch pillow that choked the life from Helen Wilson.

Unfortunately that false memory is more false than we think.

Wilson was not suffocated with a couch pillow. She was wrapped in a blanket that cut off the air around her. But in Taylors mind, that's not how it happened, because during the priming from the Gage County sheriffs department, that isn't what they told her. They told her it was a pillow.

The video ends with Taylor saying, "Wow, they got me to say I did (it). How screwed up was I?" But reacting to priming isn't screwed up. It's normal, even if the person reacting isn't.

Priming is just one example of a heuristic that effects our decision making. Other examples include:

- **Consistency heuristic** is a heuristic where a person responds to a situation in a way that allows them to remain consistent.

- **Absurdity heuristic** is an approach to a situation that is very atypical and unlikely – in other words, a situation that is absurd. This particular heuristic is applied when a claim or a belief seems silly, or seems to defy common sense.

- **Common sense** is a heuristic that is applied to a problem based on an individual's observation of a situation. It is a practical and prudent approach that is applied to a decision where the right and wrong answers seems relatively clear cut.

- **Contagion heuristic** causes an individual to avoid something that is thought to be bad or contaminated. For example, when eggs are recalled due to a salmonella outbreak, someone might apply this simple solution and decide to avoid eggs altogether to prevent sickness.

- **Availability heuristic** allows a person to judge a situation on the basis of the examples of similar situations that come to mind, allowing a person to extrapolate to the situation in which they find themselves.

- **Working backward** allows a person to solve a problem by assuming that they have already solved it, and working backward in their minds to see how such a solution might have been reached.

- **Familiarity heuristic** allows someone to approach an issue or problem based on the fact that the situation is one with which the individual is familiar, and so one should act the same way they acted in the same situation before.

- **Scarcity heuristic** is used when a particular object becomes rare or scarce. This approach suggests that if something is scarce, then it is more desirable to obtain.

- **Rule of thumb** applies a broad approach to problem solving. It is a simple heuristic that allows an individual to make an approximation without having to do exhaustive research.

- **Affect heuristic** is when an individual makes a snap judgment based on a quick impression. This heuristic views a situation quickly and decides without further research whether a thing is good or bad. Naturally, this heuristic can be both helpful and hurtful when applied in the wrong situation.

- **Authority heuristic** occurs when someone believes the opinion of a person of authority on a subject just because the individual is an authority figure. People apply this heuristic often in matters such as science, politics, and education.

List referenced from http://examples.yourdictionary.com/examples-of-heuristics.html

The authority heuristic is perhaps the most valuable and commonly manipulated of the list for the segment of society that shares the same oxytocin processing disabilities as those on the autism spectrum. Psychopaths position themselves as experts to gain the trust of unwitting victims on a very regular basis.

Buridan's ass is a philosophical paradox in which a donkey is placed the same distance between two perfectly equal bales of hay. In another version of the problem the donkey is equally hungry and thirsty and is the same distance between food and water. In the paradox the donkey can't decide what it wants more. It dies, not from malnutrition, but from an inability to choose.

In the world of the psychopath, we are the donkey and they control the hay. Only they do not think in the best interest of anyone but themselves. The outcome of any situation must eventually benefit them either socially, financially or by satisfying some urge they have.

Defining psychopaths is very difficult without the aid of functional magnetic resonance imaging, or an FMRI, and performing expensive medical procedures on every criminal suspected of psychopathy is not a reality today. So a system was developed by a man who is now considered the leading authority on psychopathy.

Dr. Bob Hare spent decades developing and teaching his now famous psychopath checklist. Aside from an FMRI, it is the gold standard for determining if a person/criminal is or is not a psychopath. It is called the Psychopath Checklist Revised or PCL-R. The PCL-R is how authorities decipher average criminals from psychopaths. The following is an overview of the characteristics from checklist.

- Glibness/superficial charm
- Grandiose sense of self-worth
- Pathological lying
- Cunning/manipulative
- Lack of remorse or guilt
- Shallow affect
- Callous/lack of empathy
- Failure to accept responsibility for own actions
- Need for stimulation/proneness to boredom
- Parasitic lifestyle
- Poor behavioral control
- Lack of realistic long-term goals
- Impulsivity
- Irresponsibility
- Juvenile delinquency
- Early behavior problems
- Revocation of conditional release
- Promiscuous sexual behavior
- Many short-term marital relationships
- Criminal versatility

Criminals are judged based on how many of the traits from the list they have and to what degree. The higher a person scores on the list, the more likely they are deemed psychopathic. Each characteristic is a spectrum, like autism, so the list can be highly subjective. As Jon Ronson outlined in his book, The Psychopath Checklist, once a person is deemed a psychopath they are widely regarded as incurable by the vast majority of psychologists and criminal justice systems.

Unfortunately we have learned the difficulties of rehabilitating psychopaths the hard way. Take the case of Norman Mailer and Jack Abbott.

In 1980 Random House signed Jack Abbott to write his book, In the Belly of the Beast. It was about his time in federal prison for charges ranging from robbery to the stabbing murder of a fellow inmate. The book would include excerpts of his letters to pen pal and fellow author Norman Mailer.

Mailer was the popular author of books such as The Naked and the Dead, The White Negro and The Executioners Song which is derived from the execution of convicted murderer Gary Gilmore. During Mailers research of criminals, he was seduced by the writing of Abbott. It was with Mailers help that Abbott not only signed his publishing contract, but was also paroled and set free. He would burst on to the literary scene a newly freed man. His freshly released book, In the Belly of the Beast, was scheduled to launch his new, free life.

On July 19th 1981, the New York Times Book Review published a review of the book. The reviewer, Terrence Des Pres, a Colgate University professor, wrote that the book was "awesome, brilliant, perversely ingenuous; its impact is indelible, and as an articulation of penal nightmare it is completely compelling."

The positive review of the book was fabulous press that didn't last long. It would be usurped by another story. A story more intriguing than one of a newly released felon with a knack for writing.

It was the story that on the morning before the review of his book was published, Jack Abbott stabbed Richard Adan in the heart. Mr. Adan was a waiter at the restaurant Abbott and two women were visiting. The fight happened when Abbott asked to use the bathroom. Mr. Adan explained to Abbott that the restroom wasn't available because the restaurant didn't have accident insurance.

So Abbott murdered him.

Abbott's positive book review ran the same day that police announced the manhunt for the him. After his capture, Abbott personified many of the traits from the PCL-R. He acted as his own lawyer; (grandiose sense of self-worth, lack of realistic long-term goals, impulsivity and irresponsibility.) He berated Mr. Adan's widow in court for crying over the loss of her husband; (lack of remorse or guilt, shallow affect, callous/lack of empathy and poor behavioral control.)

In fact, the notes from he trial read like a description of exactly how to prove one is a psychopath according to the PCL-R. Abbott even had the gaul to publish another book after the murder called My Return, for which he was promptly sued and lost $7.5 million.

But it isn't surprising that a lifelong criminal was a psychopath. It also comes as no surprise that he was able to manipulate Mailer into assisting his release from prison and his lucrative book contract.

But was Mailer manipulated?

The story, as unbelievable as it is, gets even stranger when we peek into Mailers life.

In The White Negro, Mailer wrote this about fictional young thugs murdering a shop owner.

-It can of course be suggested that it takes little courage for two strong 18-year-old hoodlums, let us say, to beat in the brains out of a candy-store keeper, and indeed the act – even by the logic of the psychopath – is not likely to prove very therapeutic, for the victim is not an immediate equal. Still, courage of a sort is necessary, for one murders not only a weak fifty-year-old man but an institution as well, one violates property, one enters into a new relation with the police and introduces a dangerous element into one's life. The hoodlum is therefore daring the unknown, and no matter how brutal the act, it is not altogether cowardly.-

It seems Mailer thought that if two strong young men, "beat in the brains out" of a weak, older candy store owner it was not cowardly, but daring. (callous/lack of empathy.) Perhaps this view of murdering the weak is what drove him to his next stunt.

On November 20th, 1960, Mailer ended an argument with his wife, Adele Morales by stabbing her in the back and chest, trying to force the two and a half inch knife into her heart, and almost succeeding.

After the stabbing he appeared at the hospital to lecture the surgeons about the dimensions of Adele's wound (grandiose sense of self-worth.) Immediately afterwards he appeared on The Mike Wallace Show to plug his mayoral candidacy, where he spoke of knives and swords as symbols of manhood (shallow affect.)

Long after the event he would complain that Morales would show off her huge scar to convince people Mailer had used a much bigger knife. After his arrest he served only 17 days in Bellevue for psychiatric evaluation, then probation for the attempted murder.

Mailer ran and lost in his race as mayor of New York City in 1969, (grandiose sense of self-worth, need for stimulation/ proneness to boredom.)

He has been quoted as saying of the stabbing that he only wanted to give his wife "a knick or two," (pathological lying cunning/manipulative.) Then in his famous argument with Gore Vidal on The Dick Cavette Show, he dismissed the whole thing saying, "we all know I stabbed my wife," (callous/lack of empathy.)

Despite the attempted murder of his own wife, Mailers silver tongue and manipulations garnered him the support of Bella Abzug and Gloria Steinem for his next political campaign.

Abzug and Steinem were women rights activists, supporting a man who tried to murder his wife, (glibness/superficial charm.)

When Mailer came the the rescue of Jack Abbott, helping launch his writing career and free him from prison, had he found untapped talent or just a kindred spirit? It's hard to argue the similarities between the two, except their standings in society.

It is also hard to argue the influence both men had over their collective worlds. One talked his way out of prison and the other never even went, dispute attempted murder. Both were very successful authors, captivating numerous people and both garnered more public support than they deserved.

It's almost impossible to deny that each man was a psychopath.

The numbers vary but Bob Hare explains that typically 1% of the general population are psychopaths. 25% of prison populations are psychopaths, but 60-70% of the violence in prison is instigated by psychopaths. That is an enormous amount of influence and persuasion.

Not all psychopaths are horrible violent murderers. As we discussed in the previous chapter, Dr. James Fallon discovered, by accident, that he is a psychopath. He has lived a very successful life.

The defining characteristic of a psychopath is not violence and bloodshed. Dr. Fallon admits that his relationships have little emotion involved. Fortunately for those around him, his urges had more to do with advancing psychology than murder.

So a psychopath, lacking adequate oxytocin processing capabilities, and those on the spectrum, who also lack oxytocin processing capabilities both wield influence because of their chemical deficiencies. Neither are shackled to the dopamine/oxytocin high produced by positive social interaction. But what differentiates the two? What makes one form of influencer positive and the other negative?

The answer could make up the content for an entire book. In chapter 7 we will use free-throws and atoms to further explain. But I think the simple answer is laid out in a quote from Dr. James Fallon, who said this,

"People with autism lack theory of mind but not empathy, while people with psychopathy lack empathy but not theory of mind."

The difference in positive influence and destructive influence is empathy.

Section 4 Humility, The Absence of Arrogance

(People with Autism Play Fewer Head Games)

Chapter 7
influence failed

"Now Moses was a very humble man, more humble than anyone else on the face of the Earth." Numbers 12:3, NIV. (Written by Moses)

One definition of head-games is psychological one-upmanship. It is the art of making ourselves out to be something we aren't to get something we want. It takes many shapes and comes in countless versions.

But it starts with arrogance.

Number 8 on our list of positive traits is that people on the spectrum play fewer head games. The real world and their reality are acceptable. They don't need to act like something they are not to gain approval.

Arrogance of a messenger has been the death nail to some of the most valuable and influential ideas on the planet. Arrogance blinds influencers to reality. Consider this story. It's a fictitious exchange between a US Navy ship and any entity the story-teller wants.

US Ship: Please divert your course 0.5 degrees to the south to avoid a collision.

CND reply: Recommend you divert your course 15 degrees to the South to avoid a collision.

US Ship: This is the Captain of a US Navy Ship. I say again, divert your course.

CND reply: No. I say again, you divert YOUR course!

US Ship: THIS IS THE AIRCRAFT CARRIER USS CORAL SEA, WE ARE A LARGE WARSHIP OF THE US NAVY. DIVERT YOUR COURSE NOW!!

CND reply: This is a lighthouse. Your call.

We like to believe that we are rational beings, only persuaded by the merits of an idea. Most of us think that good ideas spread because they are good. We are sure that bad ideas die because they are bad.

We are wrong.

Society, as a rule, does not want to change. We are invested in the beliefs and teaching we have spent decades learning. When someone shows up to change that belief, even accurately, we resist. But that resistance is more if the person is arrogant.

We are usually more comfortable being wrong with the majority of our friends, than being right with a small group of strangers. Changing our stubborn minds is very difficult. It takes two things for it to happen. A good idea, and the right person to spread that idea.

But if that great idea is attached to an arrogant person, it can die.

Alfred North Whitehead noted that, "the safest general characterization of the European philosophical tradition is that it consists of a series of footnotes to Plato."

Plato taught Aristotle, who then tutored Alexander the Great. Plato built the first organized school in the west. It was named Academes. Plato is said to be the student of Socrates. It was said that by himself, because Socrates didn't leave a written record, so Plato filled us in.

In his short time with Socrates, Plato absorbed and embraced the teachings and styles of his mentor. It is said that he loved Socrates. There was at that time, a tribe of people who loved him. One poignant example is the story of the suicide of Socrates, written by Plato from first hand accounts of his colleagues, who watched.

In 399 B. C. Socrates was tried by a jury of 500 for refusing to recognize the gods recognized by the state and for corrupting the youth. One of the youth he was accused of corrupting was Plato. 280 of the 500 Athenian jurors found him guilty.

They sentenced him to death.

He was taken to a jail where the execution would be performed and the executioner would be himself. Athenian custom was that executions were performed by drinking a cup of hemlock. The following is Plato's description of the ordered suicide of Socrates.

-When Crito heard, he signaled to the slave who was standing by. The boy went out, and returned after a few moments with the man who was to administer the poison which he brought ready mixed in a cup.

When Socrates saw him, he said, 'Now, good sir, you understand these things. What must I do?'

'Just drink it and walk around until your legs begin to feel heavy, then lie down. It will soon act.' With that he offered Socrates the cup.

The latter took it quite cheerfully without a tremor, with no change of color or expression. He just gave the man his stolid look, and asked, 'How say you, is it permissible to pledge this drink to anyone? May I?'

The answer came, 'We allow reasonable time in which to drink it.'

'I understand', he said, 'we can and must pray to the gods that our sojourn on earth will continue happy beyond the grave. This is my prayer, and may it come to pass.' With these words, he stoically drank the potion, quite readily and cheerfully.

Up till this moment most of us were able with some decency to hold back our tears, but when we saw him drinking the poison to the last drop, we could restrain ourselves no longer. In spite of myself, the tears came in floods, so that I covered my face and wept - not for him, but at my own misfortune at losing such a man as my friend. Crito, even before me, rose and went out when he could check his tears no longer.

Apollodorus was already steadily weeping, and by drying his eyes, crying again and sobbing, he affected everyone present except for Socrates himself.

He said, 'You are strange fellows; what is wrong with you? I sent the women away for this very purpose, to stop their creating such a scene. I have heard that one should die in silence. So please be quiet and keep control of yourselves.' These words made us ashamed, and we stopped crying.

Socrates walked around until he said that his legs were becoming heavy, when he lay on his back, as the attendant instructed. This fellow felt him, and then a moment later examined his feet and legs again. Squeezing a foot hard, he asked him if he felt anything. Socrates said that he did not. He did the same to his calves and, going higher, showed us that he was becoming cold and stiff. Then he felt him a last time and said that when the poison reached the heart he would be gone.

As the chill sensation got to his waist, Socrates uncovered his head (he had put something over it) and said his last words: 'Crito, we owe a cock to Asclepius. Do pay it. Don't forget.'

'Of course', said Crito. 'Do you want to say anything else?'

There was no reply to this question, but after a while he gave a slight stir, and the attendant uncovered him and examined his eyes. Then Crito saw that he was dead, he closed his mouth and eyelids.

This was the end of our friend, the best, wisest and most upright man of any that I have ever known-

Plato's hero had been forced to commit suicide over the new ideas he introduced to the community. It was a world that was ruled, scientifically and religiously by the state. What the government believed was what the people were to believe. And at that time they both believed the smallest building blocks of science were earth, air, water and fire.

Empedocles was one of the first who proposed that the building blocks of the universe were earth, water, air and fire. This was not an assumption but a truth taught by the wisest influencers.

Enter the voice of change, Democritus.

Democritus did not believe the smallest building blocks of matter were earth, wind, water and fire. Democritus believed in something much smaller.

Democritus believed in atomos, the Greek word for indivisible. Democritus taught that matter was made of atomos and void. He explained that matter was made of particles that could not be divided. He also taught that his atomos lived in an aether of nothing or void. So the chair on which you sit is not only made of chair atomos, but also small bits of nothing in between.

This was a very hard pill for the thinkers in Athens to swallow. Not the least of which being Plato, who wrote the story of the suicide of his mentor. A suicided ordered by the state for teaching new ideas. A suicide that put an abrupt end to an eight year relationship that would shape the rest of his life.

Just the idea of teaching that Socrates was wrong must have upset Plato. But there was something else about Democritus to which history eludes. A personality trait that, like in the case of Ivan the Terrible, became synonymous with the name Democritus.

Seneca explained that Democritus never appeared in public without showing his contempt for human folly. Amongst his own people, Democritus was known as "the mocker." His standard reaction to any idea or teaching that he thought wrong was to laugh at the idea or the person with the idea. His incessant laughing crept into most of the paintings and sculptures made of him.

But how did a brilliant man who, without the aid of any form of microscope explained atomic theory, allow himself to go down in history as "the mocker?"

The answer could be in a psychological bias called the false consensus effect.

The false consensus effect explains how we tend to overestimate the degree to which other people are like us. We guess that, because we like certain things, believe a certain way or understand something using certain logic, other people also think the same way.

We are all subject to the trappings of the false consensus effect. Have you ever recommended a restaurant to a friend. Then, as an exclamation of how great it is said, "everyone loves it."

Or how about this? You are shocked when someone hasn't seen your favorite movie. You scream, "who hasn't seen Avatar?"

These are examples of the false consensus effect. We think everyone is like us because we don't have time to research the actual numbers. We don't really know how many people have seen Avatar or who likes the restaurant. Our opinions are shaped by the information readily available to us, which is another heuristic. The availability heuristic.

Jan 2017 CNBC listed the 10 most dangerous jobs in America as published by the Bureau of Labor Statistics. Do you think you can guess what they are? Try to arrange the following occupations from most dangerous to least dangerous.

1. Truck Driver
2. Police Officer
3. Landscaper
4. Firefighter

Most of the people whom I offered this test came up with something like this.

1. Police Officer
2. Truck Driver
3. Firefighter
4. Landscaper

People often told me they assumed I was tricking them. So they frequently put truck driver between Police Officer and Firefighter as a safeguard. But most of them told me they actually thought Police Officer and Firefighter were numbers one and two.

That isn't even close.

In fact let me show you the full list of the ten most dangerous jobs in America.

1. Loggers
2. Fishing professionals
3. Aircraft pilots and engineers
4. Roofers
5. Trash collectors
6. Structural steel workers
7. Truck drivers
8. Farmers
9. High-voltage power line workers
10. Landscaper

Confused? Are you surprised that firefighter and police officer don't even make the list, much less in the order you thought? This is because you have been fooled by the availability heuristic.

In the generation since 9/11 we have seen the image of hero police officers and firefighters on the news, stickers, emblems and social media at a vigorous pace. These images are often accompanied by headstones, alters and phrases like 'never forget' or 'gone but not forgotten.' Because of the highly publicized deaths of the brave men and women on that day, we have been trained to believe that those two occupations are incredibly dangerous.

In reality, those professions are much safer than the jobs that we watch people do every day. Almost every day in America we have planes over our heads, have our trash collected and see a driver operating a commercial vehicle of some type.

So why do we ignore those jobs even though we are so familiar with them? Why is it so hard to put them ahead of police and firefighters on the list? Because those deaths don't get publicized the way law enforcement and firefighter deaths do. We are constantly overrun with the message that police officers and firefighter are heroes doing dangerous work, which may be true. When one of them is killed in the line of duty it makes the news and we hear about it.

But when a farmer is killed by livestock we don't hear about it. When there is construction slowing traffic on our commute home, we rarely look up to watch men hanging from poles with high-voltage power lines all around them. We just turn up the radio, cuss the truck driver in front of us and like a post on Facebook that says, "support police officers killed in the line of duty."

This programming leads to the availability heuristic that police and firefighters have some of the most dangerous jobs. We don't look up the numbers, we recall what the news or social media or our friends have told us. Most of us are absorbed in an envelope of relative sameness. And because we are so heavily influenced by our surroundings rather than the truth, we believe (usually wrongly) that most people are like us. So the false consensus effect is born.

False consensus leads to, at least closed-mindedness, at most arrogance.

Rick Barry could be the best free-throw shooter ever to have lived. At 6'7" and 205 pounds he is an imposing figure. Even as he ages beyond his 70's, he seems to carry the physical and mental agility of the aggressive athlete that he once was.

Of the top 5 best free throw shooters from the NBA, only Barry has shot over 4000 free throws and he is the only one in the NBA Hall of Fame. But he is not in the Hall of Fame strictly for great free-throws. He has been regarded as one of the best players to have ever played the game.

He was named to 12 All-Star teams. And one of the many secrets to his amazing success was, granny shots. The underhanded version of free-throws that most children start out using, but give up as soon as someone else is watching, was Rick's secret weapon.

Barry and science has proven that because of the way a players arms hang naturally at their side and the even symmetrical pressure their hands put on the ball, free throws are shot much more accurately if they are shot underhanded, rather than conventionally from a players forehead.

Peter Brancazio, physics professor emeritus from Brooklyn College says, "Judging by mechanics alone, just about every foul shot should be a winner," if a player shot underhanded. There is almost no doubt in the minds of most players and coaches that granny shots are better free throw shots. It's purely physics.

Yet for the last 50 years free throw averages have remained the same. So has the method of shooting them. Like an albatross stuck in the tar-pit of mediocrity, free throws have gone virtually unchanged for a half century. The average success rate has been right at 69 percent in the NCAA and about 75 percent for the NBA. Larry Wright, professor of statistics at Columbia, who studied the averages for the last 50 years said, "It's unbelievable. There's almost no difference. Fifty years. It's mind-boggling."

To put those numbers in perspective, Barry's all-time NBA average is 89.98% in his 15 year career.

Even with those poor numbers looming over average players, and a proven solution to the problem available, it has been nearly impossible to get anyone in the NBA or the NCAA to shoot underhanded. Barry has worked with some of the biggest names in the NBA, to influence them to shoot underhanded.

And yet, from Wilt Chamberlin to Shaq the response to Barry's advice has been a resounding no.

We are talking about one tiny change to players game that could score him, on average up to seven more points per game.

So is that a big deal? Let's look at the average, final score of the five games between the Golden State Warriors and Cleveland Cavaliers during the 2017 NBA finals. The average score of each team at the end of each game was:

Warriors 121.6 Cavs 114.8, less than seven points difference.

That means that potentially, if the Cleveland Cavaliers had one player on their team who simply shot underhanded free throws, they may have won the championship rather than lost. If the whole team chose to shoot underhanded, it would have been no contest.

Whats more, Money Nation says the difference in pay when a team wins a championship can mean 30%-50% increase in pay and endorsements. Depending on the player, that can be an extra $200,000 to $12 million more, *per year*! Just to shoot underhanded free-throws.

Yet, Rick Barry can't convince one player in the NBA to do it. Basically Rick Barry is selling winning, million dollar lottery tickets for next to nothing, and no one is buying.

As you probably guessed, the message isn't moving because of the messenger.

Allow me to share a few quotes with you about Rick Barry. Keep in mind these quotes come from some of the people closest to Rick in an article in Sports Illustrated, not from his critics.

"His teammates and his opponents generally and thoroughly detested him."

"Rick's negativity came across to the viewers."

"He was an extremely disliked individual. We'd be in a limousine together and people would pound on the windows trying to punch him in the face."

"When you've got nothing nice to say, you don't say anything at all," after being asked why he doesn't say much about Barry.

"Around the league they thought of him as the most arrogant guy ever."

And for our purposes, perhaps the most poignant quote of all, "Rick lived in a narrow sphere of influence."

Rick Barry is almost universally regarded as a complete jerk. Even in his autobiography Barry admitted that he **punched a nun**. In the same book, his mother called him greedy and his father said, "I have it on good authority that the other players jaw broke when he hit the ground, not when Rick punched him."

In the incredible podcast Malcolm Gladwell did with him, Rick Barry's arrogance comes through. Keep in mind, during the entire show Rick only speaks for less than 6 minutes.

"Watch a game," Rick's cadence speeds up. "A guy shoots free throw and misses and everybody goes up and slaps his hand.

What the, where the hell did that come from?" He's angry now.

"I want to know who the guy is that started doing that," the more he talks, the angrier he sounds, "and who was the genius that said, man that's a great idea. Let's go up and slap the guys hand and let's go up and disturb the guy's concentration when he's supposed to be focusing on shooting his free throws and worry about having to slap the hands of his teammates!"

After that he makes a comment that seems to embody who he is. He says, "plus the fact you should go up and smack him on the head for missing the free throw, not smack him on the hand and say it's okay, because it's not okay. You just cost us a point!"

It's not okay, you just cost us a point. Imagine you are a player in the NBA. Would you listen to someone who would, "smack you on the head," because, "you just cost us a point?"

If that person is one of many coaches on a team, maybe. But if he is an outsider, trying to get you to change something you have believed and worked on for decades, not a chance. Knowing you might get smacked in the head for costing us a point, you probably wouldn't care to even engage this person.

Rick's false consensus is that everyone thinks like he does about basketball. That winning is more important than relationships was a given in his life. Even though he has the secret to winning more games, he can't build the relationships he needs to spread the message.

Democritus was really only one relationship away from spreading atomic theory. If Plato, the man who started the first organized school in the west, had been his colleague, he may have had a voice. But Democritus, like Rick Barry, was not in the business of making friends. Like Rick's obsession with winning, Democritus lived to be right, and laugh at those who weren't.

Plato did not embrace Democritus. He suggested Democritus books be burned. And the society that ordered the destruction of Socrates happily destroyed the writings of "the mocker." There is no written record left today of Democritus, only that which others wrote about him. In fact, when Aristotle came along after Democritus and studied the law that matter was made of earth, air, fire and wind he only found one problem. Empedocles had left out one element, aether.

For centuries the accurate atomic theory lay dormant next the the belief that matter was made of five elements. It wasn't until 1803, when John Dalton put together his atomic theory, a millennium after Democritus died, that the ancient truth came to light.

Atomic theory was crushed just like proper free throw shooting, under the weight of arrogance. Winning WWII required one man who had a complete absence of the trait, which you'll find out about in the next chapter.

In perhaps the most arrogant footnote to the story, we named the atom after the atomos speculated upon by Democritus. The word atomos in Greek is undivided, or unable to be divided. His theory was that matter was composed of fundamental, indivisible building blocks.

When we named what we now call the atom, we were referring to what Democritus described. Of course we know now that atoms can be divided.

But Democritus didn't say that atoms are a cluster of protons, neutrons and electrons. He said that matter is made of fundamental, indivisible building blocks. Very frequently academics look over their glasses and down their nose at the same time saying, Democritus was wrong because the atom can be divided.

But we named the cluster of protons, neutrons and electrons after atomos, not him.

So who was actually wrong?

If those on the spectrum play fewer head games, and don't manipulate reality to support their own arrogance, perhaps they understand that it was us who named the atom inappropriately.

Section 4 Humility, The Absence of Arrogance

(People with Autism Play Fewer Head Games)

Chapter 8
influence achieved

"The biggest challenge after success is shutting up about it."
-Criss Jami

I have very bad news.

The world is ending.

Not only is the world ending but I know when and how. It won't be pretty, but I can show you how to manage this catastrophe. Now for the scary part, the date is. . .

This sentence has been finished inaccurately by countless fortune tellers, cult leaders and outright wackos. (Just to clarify, that is wacko as in mentally unstable person, not Waco the town in Texas where David Koresh and the Branch Dividians met their demise during a standoff with the US government.)

The scenario has played out almost the same way many times over. A charismatic leader amasses a following. They all believe in something that runs slightly contrary to the general, accepted belief. He (it's usually a man) is able to persuade the followers of this belief using a line of reasoning, or an interpretation of ancient text that supports what he preaches.

The followers rally, the movement grows and suddenly their group gains momentum. The believers begin preaching to each other, explaining how the predictions, beliefs and prophecies of the leader have played out in their own life. Now it isn't just the leader preaching the new "truth," it is everyday people teaching other, everyday people.

Then it happens. The leader has found a symbol, a sign or a message explaining the world will end. Of course the followers believe him. He no longer has the status of man, he's superhuman, a deity or a prophet.

Thanks to his status he knows exactly how the followers should handle this upcoming catastrophe. He explains the protocol for the event. Belongings are sold, modifications are made and every detail is addressed in haste to make sure the group is on the proper side of the event.

Then, on the date and time the prophet promised, it happens.

Nothing.

The sheep-headed god doesn't show up, the comet doesn't hit nor do the poles of the earth reverse abruptly.

As a result, all of the intelligent people who witnessed this silliness walk away from the cult, right? A rational person would take this a sign that the leader is wrong, wouldn't they?

Well, no.

In a blistering display of arrogance, seemingly normal people not only don't walk away from the cult, but they double down and their faith grows stronger. They refuse to admit defeat and they explain away or rationalize what happened.

Think this is an exaggeration? Let's take a look at Harold Camping.

Harold Camping was the popular Christian radio personality on the Oakland-based radio show, Family Radio. He was one of the original co-founders of the show in 1958. As an engineer, Camping drew very educated listeners, many of whom were engineers like him. The mission of he and his co-founder Dick Palmquist was to spread the Christian gospel as far and wide as possible. But almost 40 years after the founding of the show, the message took a dramatic change.

In the 1990's, Harold began interpreting the Bible. He made a few calculations and discovered that the end of the world was prophesied within the pages. Thanks to a little math and insight partnered with a lot of speculation, Camping calculated the date to be September 4, 1994, or maybe September 6. After all, no one is perfect. Hence the name of his book, 1994? (Yes, the question mark was part of the title.)

Camping convinced people to sell their homes and donate the money to the show. People cashed out their life saving and offered it up to spread the message. After all, what good is a pile of money when the world is about to end?

Then, it didn't happen. September 4 and 6, 1994 came and went with nothing more than a few TV showings of Saved by the Bell, The Fresh Prince of Bel Air and Boyz II Men songs playing on the radio.

So what was the result? Did Family Radio fold up and die after listeners learned they had given all of their money to a fraud?

In a word, no.

Between 1997 and 2011, Family Radio accepted $216 million in donations alone. This money came from a wide spectrum of listeners. Highly educated listeners to high-school dropouts supported the cause. At the time the station also enjoyed big profits from the sale of some assets.

Being flush with cash, Camping (amazingly) stumbled upon the errors in his previous calculations. He found the new calculations pointed to May 21, 2011. Now the station had over $100 million of listener money to spend on the media blitz to spread this new revelation. That was $100 million offered up freely by people who were, for the most part, completely aware of the previous failed prediction!

Again, May 21, 2011 came and went, in a non-time-ending fashoin.

Harold Camping's obituary on April 10, 2014 in the Telegraph says this about his listeners.

"Such was their generosity, that by 2011 his radio network owned 66 stations in America alone with assets worth $120 million."

If the words unthinkable, or odd come to your mind, you aren't alone. Most of us on the outside of these cults feel the same way. But if it were a one-off, strange occurrence, wouldn't it be isolated? Surely there wouldn't be more examples like this, would there?

Camping was far from the only person who bore out this cycle of predict, be wrong, grow influence.

Credonia Mwerinde predicted the end of the world on December 31, 1999. When it didn't happen, her followers stuck around because Mwerinde changed the date to May 17, 2000. On that day the world did end for many of them when, during the gathering a bomb exploded in their church. The resulting investigations found the dead from the gathering, plus over 300 previously murdered bodies under the church.

Lee Jang Rim predicted the end to 20,000 people in his South Korean church called Dami Mission. The date was to be October 28, 1992. But Rim was in prison on that date for fraud. Even still followers gave up their worldly possessions, children and even committed suicide in preparation for the event. Even though October 29, 1992 showed up as scheduled, Rim still has a following today under his new name Lee-Dap-gye.

Robert Miller founded Elohim City, which has been linked to alt-right hate groups such as the KKK and Neo-Nazis. Miller predicted the beginning of the end would be August of 1999 during a heated, international race war. Despite being incredibly wrong the church not only survived, but currently operates under the leadership of Miller's son.

What causes hoards of people to continue following such ridiculous leaders? How can such illogical actions come from often times very smart people? (Remember, a large part of Camping's audience were extremely well educated.)

The answer in layman's terms is arrogance. Scientifically it's called cognitive dissonance. Camping's irrational followers were so sure they hadn't donated their life savings to a fraud, they talked themselves into believing the unbelievable. It was easier for them to tell themselves and the world, "I wasn't wrong when I sold my house and gave the money to Camping," than it was to say, "I blew it."

They were much too arrogant to admit their mistake.

Cognitive dissonance takes many forms. Imagine the person who wants to be environmentally friendly. They recycle, grow their own vegetables, clean with green chemicals and drive a huge, gas-guzzling SUV. Yes, they drive a vehicle proven to put out more carbon and use more fuel than most. How can that be? That should be a complete contradiction to what they believe.

The market has offered these people the perfect out for their cognitive dissonance. They can buy carbon offsets to ease the mental burden they have from buying the SUV. Because they can't live with the thought of hurting the environment, they believe that buying carbon credits, which go to fund environmentally friendly projects, offsets their own environmentally harmful actions.

But it isn't true.

Yes, buying carbon credits often goes to fund positive environmental projects. But does it really offset their SUV, or private jet emissions or massive homes?

Absolutely not.

It is the equivalent of eating doughnuts today because you are going to work out extra hard tomorrow. The fact is that you can work out extra hard tomorrow without eating the doughnuts today. The doughnuts are fattening, and the SUV burns a lot of fuel, period.

You can't buy back environmental damage with carbon offsets. The damage still occurs. Buying carbon offsets is a tax on the conscious of progressives who can't live the lifestyle they preach. It is well-funded cognitive dissonance.

Cognitive dissonance is nothing more than our natural ability to tell ourselves, "the rules don't apply to me." We rationalize our decisions in the face of mounting evidence. If unchecked, develop arrogant behaviors as a result. It is very natural, hard to overcome and common to most people. But there are a few (I'm sure by now you know who they are) who don't fall into the cognitive dissonance trap.

Enigma was the most complex encryption machine of its time. It was how the German military coded their communication during WWII. It looked like a larger version of a typewriter. With a set of keys on the bottom and corresponding letters on a board above the keys. Except the upper set of letters weren't keys, they were lights. As the typist pressed a key, Enigma triggered a different letter to be typed. Then the letter that was actually typed lit up on the board above the keypad.

After a key was pressed, a rotor turned one click, changing the encryption for the next letter. This was amazingly ingenious and made the code nearly impossible to break, unlike basic encryptions.

For instance if I were to use a simple encryption to code the word book, it might look something like this.

cppl

Remember I am an author, not a code writer. The cipher for this code is that each letter of the word is written using the following letter in the alphabet. So b becomes c, o becomes p and k becomes l.

This type of encryption is simple to decode. You can plainly see there is a double letter in the middle of the word. Pair that with the fact that it is a four letter word, with the first and last letters being different from each other and it becomes fairly easy to understand the code.

But the ever-changing style of the Enigma code made that type of translation impossible. The word book would not have a double letter corresponding to the double o in the word. But the word 'type' could wind up with a double letter.

It was a huge pile of pure gibberish.

The rotor had 26 different positions. But that's not all. After the first rotor completed a full, 26 position rotation, it triggered another rotor to move one click, and the cycle was repeated 26 more times, with 26 more encryptions. Then, click, another set, then another until the second rotor completed 26 different positions. Then began the third, 26 position rotor.

All said, there were 17,000 different encryptions before the process repeated itself. But that is only if you start the machine at the beginning of the rotor cycles, which the Germans did not do.

Each day they would start by setting the rotors at different positions. Those settings were key. The Allies had Enigma machines, but without knowing what rotor positions to set the machine at for any given code, they were useless. And because the code was regulated by different rotor positions at the beginning of each day, there was a possible 159 million, million, million possible encryptions just in one day.

Then, at midnight, the Germans would change the original settings for each Enigma machine. The Allies then started the process of decoding 159 million, million, million possibilities, by hand, all over again. It was an exercise in futility. In a word, it was hopeless.

Enter a man named Alan Turing.

Alan did not fit in. In the incredible movie, The Imitation Game, which follows the story of breaking the code of Enigma, a saying comes up again and again.

"Sometimes it's the people no one imagines anything of who do the things that no one can imagine."

Alan Turing was a person who, for a time, no one imagined anything of.

From an early age, Alan did not fit the image of a young, male child in England. He was slight, quiet and obsessed with learning, especially math and science. So much that when he was 13 he was scheduled to start at the Sherborne School. It was a high level boarding school in Sherborne, 60 miles from his home in Southampton.

But the 1926 General Strike in Britain stopped business and travel, including Turing's ride to his new school. Fully encompassed in his passion for learning, Alan rode a bicycle the 60 miles, stopping halfway to stay overnight for the opportunity to attend Sherborne. Knowledge was his best friend, as long as that knowledge came in the form of math or science.

But he struggled with the classics, such as Latin. In one report his Latin teacher explained why Allan was second to last in his class this way. "He ought not to be in this form of course as far as form subjects go. He is ludicrously behind."

The headmaster of the school explained that Allan was, "the sort of boy who is bound to be a problem for any school or community."

Allan did not fit in.

During his tumultuous young adulthood he studied the work of John von Neumann and Einstein to name a few. It was work from brilliant men like these who inspired Turing to imagine greater things and to solve unsolvable problems. In his torrent of ideas he came up with the idea that would save well over 20 million lives and revolutionize the world.

The Universal Turing Machine was a large piece of hardware which could compute multiple calculations or problems that were fed into it. It was a revolution in machinery. To think that a machine could be made for the purpose of solving virtually any problem was unthinkable.

But WWII provided the opportunity for Turing to prove his machine in the form of cracking Enigma.

It was mathematically impossible for people, regardless of their intelligence, to solve a riddle with 159 million, million, million solutions every day. There simply were not enough people or time to make that happen. Turing knew that it would take a machine, with a massive computing ability to break the code.

England was suffering the burden of war. All practical commodities were being used to support the war effort. To ease the burden, the US was sending provisions across the Atlantic to replace the depleted supply.

But most of those provisions, along with the crew of the boats they were on, landed not in the UK, but in the bottom of the cold, deep ocean. German u-boats plagued the supply efforts relentlessly, and the messages directing those u-boats were floating through the air, for anyone with basic radio knowledge to intercept. But they were written in German, and coded with Enigma.

The Allies had Enigma machines. They had German translators. All they needed was the cipher, and Allan Turing built the machine (the Turing Universal Machine) that could do it. He, along with the help of a few brilliant assistants, built the answer at Bletchley Park. It could read a coded message and decode it fast enough for the Allies to take action.

The machine and Turing are credited with ending the war two years sooner that thought possible, and saving 20 million lives.

But Allan had a problem. He habitually broke one of England's most stringent laws. The Labouchere Amendment outlawed homosexuality.

From his youth, Allan identified as a homosexual. There are multiple accounts of his attraction to Christopher Morcom, a childhood friend who died as a teenager, affecting Allan deeply. It is also speculated that he attended Kings College in Cambridge because of their well-known leniency towards homosexual behavior.

But on March 31, 1954, Judge J. Fraser Harrison found Allan Turing guilty of indecency. His sentence was the option of prison, or chemical castration and probation. At this moment in time Allan Turing would have been well within his rights to choose prison. It would have been understandable if he refused to admit there was something wrong with him that needed treatment. In fact, in most court cases the defendant has a sense of cognitive dissonance, explaining away why their circumstances don't warrant punishment.

Allan did not.

He accepted the "cure" set forth by the courts. He took his court ordered prescriptions without fail. By all accounts he was a model criminal, acting in accordance to the government in their attempt to "cure" his homosexuality.

But on June 7th, 1954, just two short months later, Allan Turing was dead.

He died from eating a poisoned apple. Allan often ate an apple before bed. It was in his, very strict routine. He also was fond of Snow White and the idea of the poisoned apple in that story. His death has been officially ruled a suicide. Many have speculated he was poisoned. Neither is a fitting end to the 41 year old man, who didn't fit in, saved millions of lives and changed the world.

Chemical castration is not something we, as a society would consider a "cure" for homosexuality today. But, in classrooms and laboratories all over the world, countless people are searching for a "cure" for autism.

But whom would we cure?

Autism is a spectrum. There are those on the spectrum who suffer physically, but there are also those who only suffer socially. They are perfectly capable of living a full life. Would we "cure" the socially awkward because of how we feel about them, like Alan Turing was cured because of how society felt about him?

Of course there are those on the spectrum who would benefit greatly from a cure. But there are those who would simply lose some social quirks along with the amazing gifts that come with their specific brand of autism. They would become slaves to the interpretations of others emotions, intoxicated with fake trust from oxytocin triggered by ill meaning culprits and victims of cognitive dissonance.

Would their lives be better if they were cured?

Would "curing" autism help the patients become just as arrogant as the rest of us? "Curing" autism would perhaps infect them with the same cognitive dissonance that was missing in Alan Turing, but that the cult members had in abundance. Perhaps they would lose their influence and intelligence along with their social tick, or shy demeanor that makes neurotypicals uncomfortable.

Maybe they would be just as incompetent as the man in chapter 9, who could've stopped Bernie Madoff's ponzi scheme a decade sooner if he had the skills of someone with ASD.

As another example of the powerful influence people on the spectrum have, Allan Turing had a severe impairment of social skills, he was completely obsessed with his work, he lived by a set of routines, had many non-verbal communication problems and had some trouble with motor skills. All of which would classify someone today with Aspergers syndrome.

But in 1954, the world wasn't out to cure Aspergers or autism, they set out to cure homosexuality.

In 2017 a law was established, retroactively pardoning men convicted and "cured" of homosexuality in the UK.

It is called the Alan Turing law.

Section 5 Social Interaction

(People with Autism Live in the Moment)

Chapter 9
influence failed

"This is my letter to the world that never wrote to me."
-Emily Dickinson

Rene-Thierry Magon de la Villehuchet lost over $1.4 billion.

It wasn't all his.

In fact most of it wasn't his.

It was from friends, relatives and clients who asked him to invest their money safely. He was relied upon by everyone from his direct family members to European royalty. He was dignified and proper in the fashion of French aristocracy. He loved sailing and was always well groomed. He personified what the French upper echelon trusted.

But in 2008 that trust died, along with the billions he had invested. So 3 days before Christmas, Mr. Villehuchet locked his office door on the 22nd floor of his Manhattan office. He put his feet up on his desk and swallowed a lethal dose of pills. Just to make certain the suicide worked, he opened the veins on his left wrist and bled out into a trash can he considerately placed under his arm to contain the mess.

Just a few weeks earlier Villehuchet watched, with the rest of us, as the largest ponzi scheme in history unraveled. The numbers are still being calculated today. But when Wall Street collapsed in 2008, somewhere around $65 billion vanished. $1.4 billion of that coming directly from Villehuchet. It was gone, not because of the adjustment in the market, but because the unassuming, former chairman of the NASDAQ was running a decades-old ponzi scheme.

When authorities arrested Bernie Madoff he said, "There is no innocent explanation."

Bernard L. Madoff Investment Securities LLC opened in 1960. The company's founder looked more like a librarian than a Wall Street hustler. Bernie Madoff the man appeared quiet and humble, not the personification of a wolf or shark that seems to describe successful, cutthroat investors.

But his appearance did not stop him from being great in the beginning. The company became one of the top market makers on Wall Street. In a nutshell a market maker establishes both the buy and the sell price for a commodity or a financial product and makes money on the difference, or the spread between the two prices.

Investopia explains it this way.

-Market makers compete for customer order flows by displaying buy and sell quotations for a guaranteed number of shares. The difference between the price at which a market maker is willing to buy a security and the price at which the firm is willing to sell it is called the market maker spread. Because each market maker can either buy or sell a stock at any given time, the spread represents the market maker's profit on each trade. Once an order is received, the market maker immediately sells from its own inventory or seeks an offsetting order. There can be anywhere from four to 40 (or more) market makers for a particular stock depending on the average daily volume. The market makers play an important role in the secondary market as catalysts, particularly for enhancing stock liquidity and, therefore, for promoting long-term growth in the market.-

As an example, if the bid/ask for Facebook is $185.00/$185.05, the market maker can put in a bid for Facebook at $185.01. If everything falls into place in this scenario the market maker can sell 1000 shares of FB at $185.05 and buy them back at $185.01 making $.04 on each share or a total of $40. There is much more to it but basically this is what Madoff did on the legitimate side of his business for decades. He wrote both sides of a trade over and over again for decades. To do that you have to have someone picking up your trades and trusting that you are treating them right.

But this part of his business wasn't the problem. This all happened on the 18th floor of the Lipstick Building on Third Avenue in Manhattan. The work coming from that floor was fine. It was what Bernie was doing on the 17th floor of the same building that brought thousands to financial ruin. Bernie had a few dozen staff helping him run the largest ponzi scheme in history.

Charles Ponzi may not have invented the scam, but he made it so famous that we named it after him. He found a loophole in the mail system. During his scam, he bought international reply coupons in one country. These could be exchanged for much more expensive stamps in other countries. This turned out to be profitable for Ponzi, but when he learned that people would pay him for the initial investment of the IRC's and then share a portion of the profit after the exchange, everything changed.

Ponzi began taking investors money and spending it on himself. Then to appease the initial contributors, he would take on more investors, use their money to pay off the first investors and repeat the cycle. At one point he is credited with making $250,000/day in 1919!

As long as he had more people paying into the scheme than wanting money back, he was fine. But, as with all scams, this one collapsed. Eventually Ponzi had to pay out more than he was taking in. Too many people wanted their money back and not enough were investing to make the payment. So the scheme fell apart, Ponzi went to prison and eventually died broke in Rio de Janeiro in 1949.

Madoff was running an identical operation, only rather than being based on postage, it was based on stocks and Wall Street.

Bernie was being funded mainly by foreign banks and what are called feeder funds. Bernie Madoff did not go down to the docks and convince dock workers to invest their retirements with him. He went to the companies and banks who had already convinced the innocent dock workers to invest in their retirement packages. These funds typically don't do the investing, they pass it off to professionals.

Fairfield Sentry was the largest feeder fund, blindly supplying Madoff with mountains of cash to mishandle. They collected billions of dollars from investors and shoveled it in to the Madoff furnace. Fairfield Sentry had really only one obligation, and that was to ensure the safety of their clients money.

And they failed miserably.

They should've known better, and many people on Wall Street think they did. They turned a blind eye to their own verification policies when it came to Madoff because the "returns" were so good, but also because Madoff's fees were so low. Fairfield Sentry made higher profits by charging typical fees to their clients, but paying lower fees to Bernie. Bernie got more clients because of his "great returns" and low fees and the feeder funds kept selling his plan. Investors were convinced of the great value they were getting by the complacent feeder funds, and continued handing over their money to Bernie.

Madoff would invest it in the finer things for himself and his family. Then, when the investor wanted their money back,

Madoff would write them a check, complete with fake gains, from the money new investors were giving him. The people he paid off sung his praises to their friends, who in turn invested and the ponzi scheme was complete.

But in 2008, when the sub-prime lending bubble burst and Wall Street went into a tailspin, too many people wanted their money back. Bernie could not write those checks because not enough people were investing during the market collapse to make up the difference.

So in December of 2008 the gig was up. Mark and Andrew Madoff called the FBI and turned their father in after he allegedly admitted the fraud for the first time to them.

But, in 1999, nine years earlier, Bernie Madoff was actually caught by a small team of people. Harry Markopolos worked for Rampart, a direct competitor to Bernie Madoff. They functioned as another option for Fairfield Sentry to invest client's money, only with a little more sense than Madoff.

When the staff at Rampart saw the numbers Madoff was generating for his customers, they knew they had to find a way to compete. Markopolos was trying to build a financial product that would rival the amazing returns Madoff was claiming for his clients. When he did the math on Bernie's investments, he realized that what Madoff was offering was impossible to replicate.

Markopolos compiled his calculations, found some serious flaws in the technicalities around Madoff, and discovered a real lack of evidence that there was any trading happening at all.

So Markopolos took his information to the Securities and Exchange Commission. The SEC is the government agency charged with the task of protecting investors from fraud and investigating the snakes who steal from grandma's 401K.

Markopolos offered detailed reports from the incredibly thorough digging he did into Madoff. He offered the math that didn't work. He submitted reports that showed Madoff making money every single month for years, even when the market and all of the competition lost money. He gave them the names of people who could corroborate the information.

And in 1999 Bernie Madoff was stopped in his tracks, thanks to the information offered by this brave whistleblower.

At least that is what should have happened.

But no one at the SEC would listen to Harry Markopolos and his small team of friends. The little group of weekend sleuths created an absolute masterpiece of an investigation, but were completely ignored by the people whose job it was to actually do the investigation. At this point the Madoff ponzi scheme was estimated at a few billion dollars. Huge by most standards, but dwarfed by what was stolen when Madoff finally fell nine years later.

Markopolos wasn't done though. He had another outlet that could take down Bernie. The media in the world of investing is a small, valuable community, in which Markopolos had a few friends. MARHedge, a powerful publication in the industry at the time, charged $1000 per year for a subscription. Their readership ate up every word they published. The Wall Street Journal broke stories of corruption every chance they got. These reporting agencies loved to out criminals to their readership and Bernies victims were their readership.

So Markopolos took his story to the media.

(Insert cricket noise here.)

Over the course of the near decade of work the small team put into uncovering Madoff they were able to get exactly zero investigators, journalists, financial professionals and SEC employees to take action on their material. In fact, it is speculated that, had it not been for the sub-prime financial crisis in 2008, Madoff may still be at large. His organization collapsed, as ponzi schemes do, when too many people wanted their money back during and after the markets collapsed. It was not because of the barrage of red flags Markopolos sent to the people getting paid to listen.

But why?

This was a career making investigation, a pulitzer prize story and the retirements of millions of people. Why were the signs sent by the small team ignored?

The answer is that people listen to the messenger before they listen to the message.

Unfortunately in this case, that messenger was Harry Markopolos.

Markopolos wrote an explosive and descriptive book about the entire affair. It is aptly named, 'No One Would Listen.' The narrative is a wild braid of arrogance, paranoia and revenge mixed with the most incredible financial story of our time. The audio version of the book comes with the requisite amount of distastefulness along with a strange blend of various voices reading different portions of the book for reasons unknown.

At times the book had me cheering for the SEC. The group of government officials, charged with protecting the public who were proven to be completely inept, were often more attractive as a hero than Markopolos, who was doing their job for free.

And the book is written by Markopolos!

Here are just a few excerpts from the story as examples. He opens with the blatant truth about his work when he writes, "This, then is the complete story of how my team failed to stop the greatest financial crime in history, Bernie Madoff's ponzi scheme."

Regarding derivatives he writes, "Occasionally a situation arises in which there is a second derivative called gamma, which is the rate of change in the first derivative, delta. Don't try to understand this calculation unless you intend to trade options."

The statement seems to only have one of two purposes. Either to prime us for the eventual math required to understand Madoff's scheme, or to prove to the reader we aren't as adept at financial math as Markopolos.

Then his next sentence clears up the author's intent.

"You certainly won't need to know (the equation) to understand how Bernie Madoff successfully ran his worldwide ponzi scheme for decades."

In fact the entire purpose of the book seems to point to the complete pre-occupation Markopolos had with proving to the reader that he is brilliant, along with his own paranoia. He explains how he felt his life may have been in danger, which is understandable. But Markopolos gets very strange when describing his decision not to wear a bullet-proof vest.

-There were three things you had to be able to do to protect yourself; shoot, move and communicate. I certainly was trying to communicate. I had been trained pretty well to handle the shooting part. That left mobility, which was why I decided not to wear a bullet-proof vest. I actually tried on several different types but all of them restricted my movement. If Madoff wanted to kill me he was going to use professionals.

That meant a double tap; two bullets to the back of my head.-

This sounds silly now. Most of us have heard the story of how Madoff hung his head and gave up as quietly as possible. I'm sure in the moment Markopolos had legitimate reasons to fear for his life. But this story was written after the grandfatherly Madoff walked into handcuffs and spilled his guts. Even after we all know what a coward Bernie was, Markopolos is attempting to paint a picture of his life to resemble a scene from Boondock Saints.

In the book, Markopolos seems much too pre-occupied with stories like this to connect with the reader and help us understand what happened. It becomes clear why Markopolos wasn't able to connect with the right people during his whistleblowing. Rather than building the relationships he needed to save tens of billions of dollars, he approached these vitally important interactions with a chip on his shoulder.

Keep in mind, I arrived at this opinion by reading what he wrote about these interactions. If he comes off this arrogant and preoccupied in his own book, I wonder how bitter these interactions were in person.

Harry Markopolos wasn't a reporter serving the readership of his publication. He was a representative from a rival fund to Madoff. Looking back it is easy to think the man pointing to the largest ponzi scheme in history should've been given the floor. But at the time Madoff was well respected, a pillar of big finance. He also had a massive, successful, legitimate arm of his business which operated longer than many of his rivals had been alive. Markopolos was a preoccupied, yipping, arrogant competitor whose main complaint was that he couldn't replicate what Madoff was doing.

Here is the beginning of the first submission Markopolos made to the SEC about Bernie Madoff in 2000.

"In 25 minutes I will prove one of three scenarios regarding Madoff's hedge fund operation.

1. They are incredibly talented and or lucky and I'm an idiot for wasting your time.
2. The returns are real but they are coming from some process other than one being advertised, in which case and investigation is in order.
3. The entire case is nothing more than a ponzi scheme."

It goes on.

-My firm's marketing department has asked our investment department to duplicate Madoff's split/strike conversion strategy in hopes of duplicating their return stream. We know from bitter experience this is impossible.-

In other words, since we can't do it, no one can.

Then there is the pre-occupation Markopolos seemed to have with collecting a bounty from his whistleblowing. Many different times he has vehemently claimed that he never wanted to make a penny from Madoff. In fact, at the time of his first submission to the SEC it was not possible for him to collect a bounty from this type of case. The bounty program at the time allowed for up to 30% of funds gathered from insider trading cases to be offered to the whistleblower. But this wasn't an insider trading case. Markopolis outlines this very clearly in his book, as if to prove to us once again that he has the purest heart.

But consider the next part of his submission to the SEC.

"I would like to prove Madoff is a fraud so I don't have to listen to any more nonsense about split/strike conversions being a risk free absolute return strategy. If there is a reward for uncovering fraud, I certainly deserve to be compensated."

And, to further cloud the water he says this. Remember he is speaking directly to the SEC in this submission.

"There is no way the SEC would uncover this on their own."

His arrogance comes off very strongly when describing his first meeting with Grant Ward, the SEC Regional Director of Enforcement. He says, "As I explained this massive fraud to Ward, it very quickly became very clear he didn't understand a single word I said after hello."

At no point does Markopolos admit that perhaps it was his fault that he wasn't someone the SEC cared to hear. I came to this conclusion, just from reading his account of the investigation. I walked away believing that he is grating, arrogant and preoccupied with proving his own intelligence. Even though I believe he is intelligent and the SEC was incompetent, I completely understand why no one would listen.

As most people who have ever talked with other people know, we are mirrors to the people with whom we interact. If we put off confidence the people around us will be more confident. It we are angry our close circle will become angry. And if we are more concerned with proving we are smart and the counterpart is incompetent, that is exactly the reaction we will get from them. They will be too busy trying to prove that we are not as intelligent or right as we are acting.

Which is exactly what happened every time Harry Markopolos interacted with the SEC.

They mirrored him.

His smugness, pre-occupations and arrogance came back to him. When you need the help of the entity you are dealing with, it's best not to insult them or appear condescending.

But it isn't just giant, apathetic government bureaucracies that mirror our actions. In fact, every small twitch, gesture or even emotions very likely come back to us in social interactions. Mirroring is one of the crucial steps in building rapport. Science has uncovered what they call mirror neurons in our brain that automatically take on the speech and gestures of those around us. We act, speak and often feel similar to those with whom we interact. One of the forerunners in the study and use of mirroring was Dr. Milton Erickson.

One story has it that a 17 year old, polio stricken Erickson overheard the doctor telling his mother that Milton would not live through the next day. So he asked his mother to place a mirror in his room so he could watch one more sunset.

Fortunately for us, young Milton Erickson survived much longer than one more sunset. But the mirror remained. Eventually Milton began to notice small muscle movements of his own. He also had the time to watch people as they interacted with each other. The little twitches and movements he saw in the mirror watching himself became clear in other people. He realized that when people got in a state of rapport, they often mirrored the movements, words, tones and even breathing of each other. Eventually he used this knowledge of mirroring in his practice as a therapist. He was able to quickly build a sense of acceptance in the clients who hired him by mimicking their tone, words and gestures.

Erickson learned that these subconscious actions are powerful, which opened doors to the healing of patients through subconscious means.

Most times we aren't aware of mirroring. It doesn't matter if we are the mirror or the mirroree (not a real word,) we usually don't see it. But it happens anyway. Erickson found what scientist now know is the result of mirror neurons.

The American Pshychological Association explains it like this.

-You're walking through a park when out of nowhere, the man in front of you gets smacked by an errant Frisbee. Automatically, you recoil in sympathy. Or you're watching a race, and you feel your own heart racing with excitement as the runners vie to cross the finish line first. Or you see a woman sniff some unfamiliar food and wrinkle her nose in disgust. Suddenly, your own stomach turns at the thought of the meal.

For years, such experiences have puzzled psychologists, neuroscientists and philosophers, who've wondered why we react at such a gut level to other people's actions. How do we understand, so immediately and instinctively, their thoughts, feelings and intentions?

Now, some researchers believe that a recent discovery called mirror neurons might provide a neuroscience-based answer to those questions. Mirror neurons are a type of brain cell that respond equally when we perform an action and when we witness someone else perform the same action. They were first discovered in the early 1990s, when a team of Italian researchers found individual neurons in the brains of macaque monkeys that fired both when the monkeys grabbed an object and also when the monkeys watched another primate grab the same object.

Neuroscientist Giacomo Rizzolatti, MD, who with his colleagues at the University of Parma first identified mirror neurons, says that the neurons could help explain how and why we "read" other people's minds and feel empathy for them. If watching an action and performing that action can activate the same parts of the brain in monkeys--down to a single neuron--then it makes sense that watching an action and performing an action could also elicit the same feelings in people.

The concept might be simple, but its implications are far-reaching. Over the past decade, more research has suggested that mirror neurons might help explain not only empathy, but also autism and even the evolution of language.

In fact, psychologist V.S. Ramachandran, PhD, has called the discovery of mirror neurons one of the "single most important unpublicized stories of the decade."-

The next time you are speaking to a friend, hold your arms in a certain pose, different than theirs. You will notice that eventually they will mimic your stance. Or try to replicate their breathing pattern as you speak. If you get this right, the other person will open up, be more forthcoming and you will develop rapport almost immediately. This is just the tip of the iceberg when it comes to mirroring.

But mirroring works both ways. People not only mirror our positive actions, but our distasteful behaviors as well, and Markopolos offered heaps of distasteful actions for the SEC to mirror. His preoccupation with paranoia, arrogance and snatching a paycheck took away from the amazing story he was explaining in his book. I'm sure these distractions were evident in person as well.

Throughout the book Markopolos explains his indignation towards being blown off, but seems to be oblivious as to why it happened.

On June 20th, 2002 Markopolos traveled to Europe with Rene-Thierry Magon de la Villehuchet. He built a financial product that was to be marketed as an option for investors who had too much of their portfolio with Madoff. If they wanted to diversify, this was the vehicle. Villehuchet planned to introduce Markopolos to some of his high-level investors to consider this new option. The first meeting was to be with Prince Charles.

But Harry lost the invitation.

The following is a verbatim transcription from the account in No One Would Listen about that incident, and the entire trip afterwards.

-...(they said) they hadn't invited me to this meeting because I didn't know how to curtsy. Obviously that was their joke and so I responded, Of course I do, but by tradition Americans don't curtsy to British royalty because they have never defeated us on the battle field. That's why Americans don't bow when meeting the Queen.-

Remember, this is a man trying to convince British royalty to hand him millions, if not billions of dollars to invest in a product he created out of thin air. The product was also not offering as much of a return as Madoff, on paper. Of course that was because they actually had to produce returns from the market, not create them out of thin air like Madoff was doing. But European aristocrats didn't know that at the time.

He goes on,

-I don't think they liked my joke. I was scheduled to have dinner with the two of them that night but it never happened. In fact, throughout the entire trip, after the last meeting of the day I got kicked to the curb. We didn't eat a single dinner together. Obviously I was good enough to have breakfast and lunch with them, but I didn't make the dinner cut. I wasn't particularly pleased with that but I was polite enough not to remind them who won the Revolutionary War.-

But that last sentence isn't true. His first stupid comment was a staunch reminder of how that war ended. He said it while he was standing in their homeland, with his hand out asking for money.

Imagine how he acted while he was accusing someone of theft.

Bernie Madoff stole billions of dollars from innocent people and the SEC was complicit in the theft. They are the criminals in this situation. But Markopolos had the opportunity to shut it down at a tenth of size it became. His preoccupation with proving his own brilliance, paranoia and trying to get paid killed the influence he needed to stop the crime. He made very poor impressions around the industry, which they mirrored back to him.

If it is true that people on the spectrum live in the moment, perhaps the genius, Wall Street mathematician, Harry Markopolos could've taken a note from them. If he had realized the moments called for a smile and the offer of help, perhaps the smile and help would have been mirrored back in the same manner. If he had been more focused and present, perhaps billions of dollars would not have been lost.

If he had the skill of the con-man in the next chapter, there is no doubt the money would have been saved.

Section 5 Social Interaction

(People with Autism Live in the Moment)

Chapter 10
influence achieved

"People arrive at what is attractive." -Blaise Pasquale

The phone rang in the Los Angeles office of detective George Mueller. He was the square-jawed, straight shooting detective who had just missed making a huge arrest. Cristophe Rocancourt left behind a pistol, a real, but swindled U.S. passport and a trail of famous and wealthy victims from the Hamptons to Hollywood.

But the case was about to heat up again, because on the other end of the phone was the crook he had recently missed. Cristophe Rocancourt was on the line, asking to speak with detective George Mueller.

He explained to detective Mueller that, despite mounting evidence against him, and the fact that Mueller had just missed him, he would be moving back to Los Angeles. The con-man called the detective "a good player," in a thick, French accent. He explained that they both were, "good players." He told Mueller that if the two sat down for a meal they would like each other.

Mueller was so close to capturing Rocancourt previously that the room Mueller searched still smelled of the fraudster. He had barely eluded capture by leaving the U.S. on a lavish tour of Asia with a French fashion designer named Charles Glenn.

Rocancourt told the detective about his plan to walk right back into the investigation from which he ran. In his thick, French accent he said, "If you do arrest me I'll just bail out and flee the country anyway."

He was right. That is exactly what happened.

In the summer of 2000, Rocancourt blew through the the U.S. on a whirlwind tour of lavish lifestyle and lucrative deceit. He adopted the name Rockefeller on a whim, but in an instant he found the source of his next con.

In an interview with Dateline's Mike Taibbi, Rocancourt explained that when people heard the name Rockefeller they, "melted like ice cream." It was what he counted on when he met Kim Curry and her fiancé. This is how it's explained in the Dateline interview.

-**Narrator:** Kim Curry and her fiancé, who had taken a hit in the stock market that summer, were thrilled. Christopher told them the deal was simple— they put up some money, he would invest it, they would get a tenfold profit guaranteed. So they ponied up the $50,000.

Curry: The way he presented it was this, "You give me $50,000, I will invest this money, I will in turn give you $500,000 back."

Mike Taibbi, Dateline correspondent: And when would your fiancé and you get this $500,000?

Curry: Immediately.

Narrator: It was Kim's friend, Corrine Eeltink who'd first met the young Rockefeller at a Hamptons gym, noticing that last name and that he'd signed the register with a Fifth Avenue address. And when Corrine was invited to one of Christopher's lavish dinners, he'd invited her to make a similar investment — the same sort of terms and the same knockout payoff.

Corrine Eeltink: We'll start right today with $25,000 investment.

Taibbi: How much did he say you would make with your $25,000 investment?

Eeltink: Around a million and up, in over like three months.

Narrator: Corrine bought in too. Christopher also promised millions to a real estate agent who showed him a $9 million oceanfront estate in the Hamptons. The realtor was so impressed she gave the French Rockefeller $100,000 of her own savings to invest.-

But how does a man pretending to be wealthy trick people into giving *him* money? What could possibly drive someone to write a check to a Rockefeller? One answer Rocancourt gave during the same interview shines a light on how he thought of it. His English is so poor that even the subtitles can be hard to understand.

But his intent is not.

Rocancourt: How you for a minute can be serious to think when you don't have to know history to say, "Hey, Rockefeller, your French accent. There's no Rockefeller in France." C'mon, use your brain.

Taibbi: All they needed to believe it for was a split second that if they could smell money.

Rocancourt: They smell the money like the shark smell the blood. Nothing else.

Narrator: He says he always counted on his victims thinking they were taking advantage of him, and that he always counted on their greed.

Rocancourt: You do think for that time you are much smarter than me. You did think for that time, you can profit better with me.

Taibbi: Right, and so for those people, they should be punished?

Rocancourt: No, no, no, no, no. You been a dummy. You been stupid. Just like I did prison time. I take my time. Just accept it for fact. You're not that bright. You been stupid for that time. Just accept it. Oh, you been ripped off. Is what happened.

Taibbi: But what you have done is criminal. You admit that.

Rocancourt: No question.

Taibbi: But you're saying you don't feel any sympathy for the people who lost money.

Rocancourt: No.

Taibbi: --because they were greedy and they believed in you and they threw money at you. And you didn't pay 'em back. You don't feel sorry for them?

Rocancourt: No. I keep it real. You want honesty? You have it. I keep it real. What do you want me to tell you? I have a feeling I don't have? I don't.-

Were Rocancourt's victims greedy or was the con man just playing on a little-known psychological quirk that most of us have?

The Rockefeller name is synonymous with money. Most of us would jump at the chance to let a Rockefeller invest for us. In fact it was Kim Curry who asked Cristophe if he had any investment tips. Rocancourt did not instigate the conversation. That one question was the catalyst for their loss of $50,000. She was, as Cristophe put it, smelling the money like sharks smell blood.

But when we are struggling, sometimes its our own blood we think we can smell. And so desperation holds sway and we jump on the first opportunity we can find. Like Kim, most of us wouldn't go home and research the Rockefeller name if we needed money and felt an opportunity was available. After all, we are smart enough to know what the name Rockefeller means.

Or are we?

After the Civil War in the US, a massive cultural shift happened. Whale oil was no longer the standard for lighting homes. So the black gold boom of petroleum tore through the country, and essentially the world.

John D. Rockefeller was there, selling oil through his Standard Oil Company from the beginning. His company grew so large, that on May 15, 1911 the U.S. Supreme Court ordered the company broken up in an attempt to crush the monopoly Rockefeller had on oil and money.

John amassed the largest fortune ever owned in modern times. At his death in 1937, his net worth was $340 billion. Adjusted for inflation, his fortune was the equivalent of around $600 billion today.

To put that in perspective, Forbes Magazine outlined the richest people in the world in December of 2017. In the article they explain that Jeff Bezos had surpassed Bill Gates as the richest man in the world that July, as his net worth rose to over $90 billion. If we make all things equal, the richest person alive today only has 15% of what Rockefeller had.

Rockefeller died in 1937 and his family tree is very accessible. A quick look today reveals that his namesakes are largely contained the northeastern states of the U.S.

But Rocancourt was so French, he could barely speak English. Even today, decades after the facade, Rocancourt offers interviews to media outlets. Those interviews still require subtitles because his accent is, at times, indiscernible. How did this very French man get away telling Americans that he was the French Rockefeller?

Because that is just what they wanted him to be.

Rockancourt ran his con in Hollywood and the Hamptons on purpose. These are places associated, justly or not, with selfishness and greed. In his mind he thought the people there were shallow and only out for themselves. He thought they would accept a Rockefeller into the community, not out of kindness, but because he could do something for them.

Which they did.

In the Hamptons he offered people outrageous returns if they invested their money with him. Remember, he promised Kim Curry that he could turn $50,000 into $500k in months. She was not looking at Rocancourt as a friend, she saw an extra $450,000. After all, he was only there a few months when she handed him the money. They weren't long-time friends.

In Hollywood it was a different story. He promised Tinseltown that he could get fallen stars back on track. His new friends, Mickey Rourke and Jean Claude Van Damme were guests at his dinner table, drawn to the promise of another run at a rich career, not the promise of a good friend.

In other words, like any good con-man, he found what people wanted and exploited it. But how did a pompous Frenchman fake his way into the hearts of the well-to-do so quickly just by faking a Rockefeller pedigree?

It was with a psychological nuance called the conformation bias, and it is powerful.

Conformation bias happens when we make choices that supports our preconceived notions or desires, and it happens a lot more than we think.

Science Daily explains it this way.

-The conformation bias is a tendency to search for or interpret information in a way that confirms one's preconceptions, leading to statistical errors.-

We think that what we think is right. We talk ourselves into the choices that support what we want to believe, and it happens in a instant. If we could talk openly about your last vote, it probably fell along the lines of the party or culture with whom you identify. I doubt you got out your calculator, researched the taxes and cultural repercussions and voted according to the numbers.

It's probably true that you were raised with certain political leanings, your friends lean that way and you vote mostly that way. Perhaps you think you believe in less government, but police and military are government and you want more of that. Maybe you perceive that you want to help the poor, but you vote for more funding and policies that have proven to hurt, not help the less fortunate.

Perhaps you think the car you drive is a good choice, but is it? Or is it just a reflection of the story you have chosen to believe? Do you drive a cheap car because you feel broke, even though you spend more money fixing it each month than you would on a small car payment? Perhaps you drive a giant lifted truck that rarely goes off-road because you are a guy with a beard and a gun and the truck fits your story, not your life. If you drove a car, you'd have much more money to spend on guns, but a guy in an Avalon with a beard and a pistol doesn't seem right to you.

There are countless examples of the conformation bias. We think that we make choices based on logic and reason. But we don't. We form opinions first, then make choices and stories that support those opinions, not the other way around.

The people at verywell.com wrote a great explanation of conformation bias. I have included parts of it here.

-Where do your beliefs and opinions come from? If you are like most people, you probably like to think that your beliefs are the result of years of experience and objective analysis of the information you have available. The reality is that all of us are susceptible to a tricky problem known as a confirmation bias.

While we like to imagine that our beliefs are rational, logical, and objective, the fact is that our ideas are often based on paying attention to the information that upholds our ideas.

At the same time, we tend to ignore the information that challenges our existing beliefs.

Understanding Confirmation Bias
A confirmation bias is a type of cognitive bias that involves favoring information which confirms previously existing beliefs or biases.

For example, imagine that a person holds a belief that left-handed people are more creative than right-handed people. Whenever this person encounters a person that is both left-handed and creative, they place greater importance on this "evidence" that supports what they already believe. This individual might even seek "proof" that further backs up this belief while discounting examples that do not support the idea.

Confirmation biases impact how people gather information, but they also influence how we interpret and recall information.

For example, people who support or oppose a particular issue will not only seek information to support it, they will also interpret news stories in a way that upholds their existing ideas.

They will also remember things in a way that reinforces these attitudes.

The Impact of Confirmation Biases
In the 1960s, cognitive psychologist Peter Cathcart Wason conducted a number of experiments known as Wason's Rule Discovery Task. He demonstrated that people have a tendency to seek information that confirms their existing beliefs. Unfortunately, this type of bias can prevent us from looking at situations objectively. It can also influence the decisions we make and can lead to poor or faulty choices.

During an election season, for example, people tend to seek positive information that paints their favored candidates in a good light. They will also look for information that casts the opposing candidate in a negative light.

By not seeking out objective facts, interpreting information in a way that only supports their existing beliefs, and only remembering details that uphold these beliefs, they often miss important information.

These details and facts might have otherwise influenced their decision on which candidate to support.

Observations by Psychologists
In his book, "Research in Psychology: Methods and Design," C. James Goodwin gives a great example of confirmation bias as it applies to extrasensory perception.

-Persons believing in extrasensory perception (ESP) will keep close track of instances when they were 'thinking about Mom, and then the phone rang and it was her!' Yet they ignore the far more numerous times when (a) they were thinking about Mom and she didn't call and (b) they weren't thinking about Mom and she did call. They also fail to recognize that if they talk to Mom about every two weeks, their frequency of "thinking about Mom" will increase near the end of the two-week-interval, thereby increasing the frequency of a 'hit.'-

As Catherine A. Sanderson points out in her book, "Social Psychology," confirmation bias also helps form and re-confirm stereotypes we have about people.

-We also ignore information that disputes our expectations. We are more likely to remember (and repeat) stereotype-consistent information and to forget or ignore stereotype-inconsistent information, which is one-way stereotypes are maintained even in the face of disconfirming evidence. If you learn that your new Canadian friend hates hockey, loves sailing and that your new Mexican friend hates spicy foods and loves rap music, you are less likely to remember this new stereotype-inconsistent information.-

Conformation bias is the reason that living in the moment is such an influential trait. When we are fully engaged and present in a situation it creates a bias in people that is irresistible. Those biases are made up of tiny moments, not calculated informations.

Think of a friend whom you consider honest. Do you think that because you have surveyed the people with whom they associate and they all have told stories of your friends honesty? Have you calculated the number of times they lied and subtracted it form the number of times they were honest? Or do you think they are honest because you watched them act honestly in just a few moments?

Usually if we see someone return to a store with an item for which they haven't paid just to make it right, that one incident is enough to cement them in our minds as an honest person. If someone told you that your honest friend had lied to them, would you believe them? Probably not, but your opinion is based on a very small sliver of information. One instant in time secures your premonition that they are honest. This is conformation bias.

Conformation bias also explains why when we meet someone named Rockefeller who claims to have money, we ignore the heavy French accent, or other lack of evidence to support the belief. If we want to meet a person that can make us rich, we ignore the signs of fraud.

It was this living in the moment that caused so many people like Mickey Rourke and Jean Claude Van Damme to believe there was a French Rockefeller. It was also being with Rocancourt that made them believe. In his mind, he was not acting. He was fully engaged. He was, like our friends on the spectrum, living in the moment, and in those moments, Rocancourt was the French Rockefeller.

But it wouldn't last long.

When Christophe Rocancourt was arrested on April 26, 2001 he was wearing a Rolex watch worth $28k. He was also holding receipts for two more watches totaling $148,450. This time the French Rockefeller would not avoid prison, although it wouldn't be a long sentence.

In September 2003, Rocancourt accepted a plea deal for some of his crimes. The plea resulted in a fine of $9 million, an order to pay $1.2 million in restitution and a term of three years and ten months in federal prison. Upon his release, he was the toast of France. He was the man who used American greed against them.

His intriguing life spurred the media into action. Rocancourt started a clothing line, wrote multiple books and was even cast as a leading actor in a film with Naomi Campbell. This was hardly the post prison reaction the authorities imagined when they tried Rocancourt.

But the prosecution had a difficult time finding victims who would come forward. Many were embarrassed. They knew they were somewhat viable in the fraud and did not want to come forward. It was hard for them to admit that the conformation bias they felt for the name Rockefeller was stronger than their own logic. But for most of us, that would be the case. Most of us just don't meet people named Rockefeller often.

But Rocancourt did not change his stripes.

In July 2009, French filmmaker Catherine Breillat accused Rocancourt of scamming her out of 700,000 €. Breillat, who was diagnosed with a cerebrovascular disease, believes Rocancourt took advantage of her because of her disability. As a result of this accusation, the film Bad Love, with Rocancourt and model Naomi Campbell, was cancelled.

Breillat explained to a French journalist that her first meeting with Rocancourt may have been the worst day of her life. She says it was even worse than the day she was diagnosed with her disease. In 2012, Rocancourt was convicted of abus de faiblesse (abuse of weakness) for this crime, and sentenced to a short stay in prison once again.

The name con-man is short for confidence man. Because in the small moments of the scam they must have all the confidence in the world that the story they are selling is real. If that confidence catches on to other people, they will believe the lie because of the conformation bias.

The conformation bias set in to help those victims believe that a Rockefeller could make them rich. Not unlike some of the "victims" from the Bernie Madoff ponzi scheme. Fairfield Sentry knew Bernies returns couldn't be real. But they had a conformation bias towards him. They were "making" so much money from Bernie that they wanted what he was selling to be true, even when they should have known that it wasn't.

Living in the moment is an incredibly persuasive trait. It leads people to a conformation bias that heavily favors trust and cooperation. Those on the spectrum who naturally do this have a powerful tool that most of us lack. It allows them to take advantage of those with learned helplessness, which we will discuss next.

If Harry Markopolos was fully present, like Cristophe Rocancourt, in the moments he tried to persuade the SEC of the Madoff scheme, maybe he would've had some influence, like the phony French Rockefeller had.

Section 6 How The Few Influence The Many

(People With Autism Open New Doors for Neurotypicals)

Chapter 11
influence failed

"Worldly wisdom teaches that it is better for reputation to fail conventionally than to succeed unconventionally.
-John Maynard Keynes

The word cork means so many things.

Cork is a device for plugging holes, a porous texture and a color in the family of brown. It takes context to know which meaning the word has in a sentence.

Until 2001, the phrase nine eleven had different meanings as well.

It could conjure thoughts of the iconic Porsche 911 in Carmine Red. It might have made people consider the emergency phone number system implemented in the late 1960's in the U.S.

But now the phrase causes most people to imagine two planes crashing into the World Trade Center Towers. Like me, most people see the images of people fleeing in the streets as the giants of finance crumble to the earth and melt from the skyline.

The terrorist attacks on September 11th, 2001 caused a huge ripple in the sea that is the world. For those of us who were raising young families during that time, it shook our feeling of security and safety to it's core. We wondered what the world would look like when our children matured. Would the U.S. still exist as it did that day, and just how long would this new war, fought for old reasons last?

It was a defining moment in the lives of Generation X. Up to that point the Challenger disaster, Rodney King riots, O.J. Simpson trial and the Clinton/Lewinsky scandal were likely the most memorable events of our lives.

But 9/11 changed everything.

Suddenly we were thrust into politics, religion and chaos. We had never witnessed an event that killed thousands of people in a single day. We had never seen the beginning of a war of that scale. We never had so many unanswered questions dumped upon us in such a short amount of time.

One of those questions, which was asked over and over again was, "How could this happen?"

It seems the answer was simple.

CNN breaks down the timeline this way.

September 11, 2001 - Nineteen men hijack four commercial airlines loaded with fuel for cross country flights, to carry out a terrorist attack on the United States orchestrated by al-Qaeda leader Osama bin Laden.

-- 8:46 a.m. ET (approx.) - American Airlines Flight 11 (traveling from Boston to Los Angeles) strikes the North Tower of the World Trade Center in New York City. The plane is piloted by plot leader Mohamed Atta.

-- 9:03 a.m. ET (approx.) - United Airlines Flight 175 (traveling from Boston to Los Angeles) strikes the South Tower of the World Trade Center in New York City. The plane is piloted by hijacker Marwan al-Shehhi.

-- 9:37 a.m. ET (approx.) - American Airlines Flight 77 (traveling from Dulles, Virginia, to Los Angeles) strikes the

Pentagon Building in Washington, DC. The plane is piloted by hijacker Hani Hanjour.

-- 10:03 a.m. ET (approx.) - United Airlines Flight 93 (traveling from Newark, New Jersey, to San Francisco) crashes in a field in Shanksville, Pennsylvania. The plane is piloted by hijacker Ziad Jarrah.

That was technically what happened.

But the question is not in reference to the timeline of the day. The question is in reference to the fact that 19, highly unskilled and very questionable men walked through multiple lines of security offered by the U.S. government and killed thousands of people on American soil, with almost no trouble.

How did **that** happen?

With the CIA operating mainly out of the country and the FBI functioning inside our boundaries, and utilizing a budget of tens of billions of dollars, how did 19 guys with box cutters accomplish such a heinous crime?

The answer is they walked through a psychological hole that existed within the agencies. It is not an oddity or rare. In fact it something for which most of us have the capacity. This quirk was best demonstrated and discovered in an experiment on how animals relate one thing with another.

1965 was not a good year to be a test animal. Martin Seligman was much crueler to dogs than would be allowed today. His test started by ringing a bell, then shocking a dog immediately thereafter. He was attempting to prove the association the dogs developed with the bell and the pain of the shock, which he did. Eventually the dogs would flinch from he sound of the bell, even if no shock was administered.

But the second part of the test was the most interesting.

He built a large pen with a short wall dividing the pen into two sides. The wall was short enough for the dogs to see and step over easily. Seligman then placed a dog on one side of the pen. The floor of that side had been set up to become electrified. He administered a shock to the dogs and what happened next was, well, shocking.

If the dog had previously been jolted during the bell experiment, it would just lay down and take the shock. During the bell experiment the dog had no control over the treatment. It had learned that the shocks were out of it's control. In the dog's mind there was nothing it could do to stop the pain. So it would just lie down until the shock ended.

If the dog had not been shocked it would simply jump to the other side of the pen, safe and happy. What Seligman uncovered was what he coined learned helplessness. Seligman had unknowingly trained those dogs to believe the shocks were a condition of existing. The dogs thought there was nothing they could do to stop the shock. So even when there was a clear and available opportunity to leave, they did not.

They had learned to be helpless.

In the decades following the research, learned helplessness has also been found in humans.

If we have been taught or trained that nothing we do matters, we will react accordingly and do nothing. We feel it's impossible to affect change or find something better, so we sit in the painful situation, hoping it will go away. We find ways to cope with the feeling of helplessness in the form of mood-altering chemicals, hobbies or sayings to occupy our mind and make us believe we are not in control. Things like, "the rich get richer," or "if it's meant to be, it's meant to be," and "if it weren't for bad luck I'd have no luck at all" lead to the same learned helplessness the dogs felt.

The outcomes of situations are often what causes pain in humans. The death of a friend, the loss of a place to live after losing a job or the end of a relationship that we wanted to keep hurt us deeply. Negative outcomes to situations are the source of most human suffering. But it is what we think about those outcomes that determine our mental state.

It is in the moment when we assign blame for the situation that we determine our perspective on what happened. That moment when we attribute reasons for the situation shapes everything. Psychologists have found many types of these attributions, but there are three that we use with devastating results. They result in learned helplessness. These attributes are:

1. **Internal**

Internal attributions name the person for the outcome, and nothing else.

2. **Stable**

Stable attributions are attributions that don't change with time.

3. **Global**

Global attributions don't change across situations.

For example, if a person loses their job, they may assign many reasons as to why it happened. They may think it's because they are incompetent, their boss was a bad leader or the industry is dying.

An internal attribution to that outcome is that the person who was fired is incompetent. If that person feels they are incompetent, all responsibilities for the outcome lie within the person. That internal attribution can be the beginning of learned helplessness. If the problem lies solely within the victim of the outcome, the same results are bound to follow that person to the next job, so why try?

If the attribution was that the boss was a bad leader, that would be an external attribution. That reason stays with the lost job, not with the person; making a new job a decent solution to the problem. External attributions don't usually lead to learned helplessness.

That person being incompetent, or the boss being a bad leader is not, however an example of a stable attribution. One can be better trained, competent in a different field or work for a better boss. But, if they attribute their skin color or gender to the loss, that is a stable attribution. Those are things that aren't likely to change.

A global attribution would be that the person was working at a store which became obsolete, like a record store. Globally, the industry of analog music decomposed to digital music. The industry of any type of physical music such as CD's is all but gone. If the attribution to the job loss is that the record business is dying, it would be a global attribution. If the person assigns that along with an internal attribution that the only thing they know is the record business, it is a recipe for learned helplessness.

Learned helplessness is the mindset that causes people to continue doing something that will never get them the results they want. If the person who lost their job thinks the record industry is dying and they won't go to another industry, they are helpless. But there are better, realistic examples of learned helplessness. For instance, learned helplessness is the reason American football teams still punt on fourth down.

In American football the team with the ball has four chances to move it ten yards. If the team reaches or exceeds ten yards at any time, those four chances, or downs, start over. If they don't move ten yards or more in four downs the other team gets the ball right where the fourth play stopped.

Given that the other team may get the ball anyway after fourth down, most teams choose to punt, or kick the ball away on fourth down. In other words the team gives up the chance to complete the full ten yards, or even an opportunity to score, so they can put the other team in worse field position on the next play. This puts the ball as far away from their end zone, where the other team scores, as possible. So punting should make it more difficult for the other team to score.

But the math says that isn't true.

The numbers are complicated, but essentially every yard on the field is given a value relative to the potential the team has of scoring from that position. When an astute coach factors in the potential they have of completing the full ten yards with the field position of the other team after a punt, it becomes very clear that punting is a bad idea almost always. Not only is the team giving away 25% of their chance to score, but they are doing it to put the other team in a field position that almost never equates to a big change.

If the other team had to start the next play from where the ball landed on the field it may be a different story. But that isn't the case. The other team catches the ball and then runs it back from whence it came. This return of the ball back towards the end zone, plus the loss of 1 out of 4 chances to score makes for devastating math.

This is not a theory, but is proven mathematically, and functionally on the field. But teams still punt, like addicts who need a fix. This research has been around a long time and most professional coaches have at least heard of it.

Yet they still kick away the football on fourth down.

David Romer of the University of California, Berkeley and National Bureau of Economic Research who did the research that resulted in this unconventional bit of wisdom thinks he knows why. He says that in the moment the coach chooses to kick the ball away, they are not thinking about winning. They are thinking about their job. He explains that if the team acts conventionally and loses, the coach can blame the players for the loss. But if they act unconventionally and lose, he carries the burden. So, out of fear and learned helplessness, coaches continue doing what they've always done, which is wrong.

Well, most coaches anyway.

In 2015, the Kansas City Star wrote an article about a "radical" coach who had changed his philosophy on how the game of football should be played. Coach Kevin Kelly adopted the concept to great results. The article was written early in the season, before the results could be established. But they were fascinated with the radical coach Kelly who was defying the status quo. They explained him this way.

-Kelley, the head coach at Pulaski Academy in Little Rock since 2003, has won four state titles using his radical brand of football. You've probably heard the story: Kelley's teams never punts — save for the most extreme situations. They always onside kick. And they generally treat football games like one never-ending, hair-ablaze two-minute drill. Kelley's strategies — and their subsequent success — have made him a cult figure in football circles.

He is a constant media curiosity — commanding recent profiles from HBO's "Real Sports," the Washington Post, Sports Illustrated and pretty much every publication that enjoys weird sports stories. He is adored on the Internet. (Twitter is obsessed with many things, but it LOVES coaches who never punt.) And he has become a fascination in the upper echelon of football. Earlier this year, according to the Post, Kelley scored a one-on-one meeting with former Chiefs general manager Scott Pioli, who now works for the Atlanta Falcons.

But for all the attention, Kelley has remained something of a loner — a one-man revolution against the punting fascists of the football world.-

A idea is only newsworthy if it's rare. And it stays a rare idea when the majority of people would rather sit in the pain of what is wrong than jump to the freedom of success. In the midst of learned helplessness, good ideas like not punting seem radical.

Learned helplessness can cause dogs to sit through a shock, coaches to keep doing what doesn't work and huge government agencies to shrug their shoulders and say, "that's the way it is around here," in the face of mounting evidence that danger is coming.

Doug Miller was an FBI agent assigned to the CIA's Alec Station unit. It was the unit assigned to monitoring Osama bin Laden prior to 9/11. Miller was concerned that Khalid al-Mihdhar who was a known terrorist had obtained passage to the US.

But his bosses at the CIA were not.

On Sept 11, al-Mihdhar would help fly American Airlines Flight 77 into the Pentagon.

20 months earlier, on January 5, 2000, Doug Miller learned that Khalid al-Mihdhar had a U.S. visa. In December of the previous year the CIA tapped the phone in Yemen belonging

to al-Mihdhar which began the snowball of information on him, including his possible link to an attack in 1998 on the East African embassy. So Doug Miller wrote a memo intended for the FBI, explaining that a known terrorist with ties to Al-Queada had a U.S. passport and could be headed to the US.

Because the CIA manages foreign matters and the FBI is in charge of domestic issues, this seems the logical course of action. This terrorist is about to leave foreign soil and land right in FBI jurisdiction.

But a CIA officer named Michael Anne Casey blocked the letter from going to the FBI with a note saying, 'pls hold off for now per Tom Wilshire' who was deputy chief of Alec Station. Miller was also told that this wasn't a matter for the FBI. These reactions were the exact opposite of what should have happened. CNN explained the dichotomous event this way.

- . . . according to FBI agent Doug Miller who was assigned to the same station, Alec Station (a specific CIA branch that monitored Al-Queda) that director Tom Wilshire CIA was, Tom stopped a cable from Doug that would have relayed information about two top terrorists entering southern California for three months, a crucial hand off to the FBI that usually occurs for every terrorist they know of that is entering the USA. Tom Wilshire stopped the transfer of information, and did so on purpose. Tom had a reason, yet, is failing to reveal what that reason is or why he did it. It was definitely done intentionally.-

Enter Mark Rossini.

Mark was an FBI agent temporarily working with Alec Station at the same time as Miller. He was aware Casey and Wilshire blocked the memo and became furious. Rossini was so concerned that the information was blocked, he questioned

Casey about the memo personally. In the explanation of events in historycommons.com, Rossini's interaction with Casey is described this way.

-According to author James Bamford, Rossini was "perplexed and outraged that the CIA would forbid the bureau's notification on a matter so important." Rossini will later say: "So the next day I went to her and said: 'What's with Doug's cable? You've got to tell the bureau about this.' She put her hand on her hip and said: 'Look, the next attack is going to happen in Southeast Asia—it's not the bureau's jurisdiction. When we want the FBI to know about it, we'll let them know. But the next bin Laden attack's going to happen in Southeast Asia.'" Rossini protests, saying, "They're here!" and, "It *is* FBI business," but to no avail. Even though he is an FBI agent, he cannot pass on notification to the bureau without permission from his superiors at Alec Station.-

And so, the term nine-eleven became a moniker for a horrible tragedy, that now seems to have been preventable.

Why did Casey and Wilshire stop this flow of this life-saving information?

In the years that have followed 9/11 there have been many theories. There is the the logical concept that the CIA was attempting to recruit high-ranking members of Al-Queada as double agents, and didn't want the FBI interfering. Then there is the Truther movement, a fraction of the population who think the US orchestrated the attacks.

There was even a segment of the Truther's called the No Planer's who believe the planes were actually holograms surrounding missiles fired by the US. This group seemed loosely lead by a man named David Shayler. He is a former British MI5 agent who has a strange resume to say the least.

Shayler blew the whistle on devious and illegal activity within MI5 and was considered somewhat of a British hero for a time. But he has since been arrested, dressed as a woman going by the name of Delores Kane and then claimed to be the Messiah.

Despite the reason, the CIA did have an issue sharing certain, crucial information with the FBI. To the point that when the voice of reason spoke up in the form of Mark Rossini, it was swiftly silenced by the dominant culture of secrecy. "This is how we do things," is a dangerous result of learned helplessness that happens in humans.

Especially humans who have been deeply trained that protocol is life, such as CIA and FBI agents.

A note explaining that a terrorist has landed on US soil that must be approved before it is sent to those responsible for protecting the US, is a form of learned helplessness. It is the dog lying in the misery, rather than stepping over the wall into safety.

We are influenced by a very select few. But it is up to us to choose whose influence we follow. If we listen to the learned helplessness from conventional coaches and CIA staff who act because 'that's the way we do things,' we are bound for mediocrity, or worse. But if we pay attention to the Kevin Kelly's and the Mark Rossini's who clearly have good ideas, if we let in the 'outsiders' and value their perspective, we are bound to make better choices, and a better world.

We don't need more influencers. We have them all around us. It is whom we choose to follow that needs evaluation. Kevin Kelly and Mark Rossini opened doors for the rest of us, just like those with ASD do.

But we often choose not to enter.

Perhaps the new perspectives on life is what cultures like that of Ivan the Terrible's Russia appreciated in those with autism, but we don't.

In chapter 12 we will learn what exactly causes groups of people to act together, and possibly learn how to change.

Section 6 How The Few Influence The Many

(People With Autism Open New Doors for Neurotypicals)

Chapter 12
influence achieved

"If everyone is thinking alike, then somebody isn't thinking."
-George S. Patton.

Would you trust the same bank that held money for the Queen of England?

What about a bank that survived WWI, WWII, the French Revolution, and the Napoleonic Wars?

Would you feel comfortable having a checking account at the same bank that financed the Louisiana purchase?

If you said yes, you would have been correct, for over 230 years. For two centuries you could've slept peacefully knowing that one of the most stable financial institutions in the world was looking after your hard-earned money.

That is until January 16th, 1995.

On that day this British behemoth of money and history was shaken to death by an earthquake. Not physically as in the earthquake reduced the building to a pile of rubble. In fact that would have been a simple fix for the good people at Barings Bank. The earthquake that figuratively piled up Great Britain's Barings Bank happened in Kobe Japan.

Other than exposing the steel and concrete foundations of buildings and fissures in the Japanese ground, the earthquake also exposed a single man, whose fraud and deceit went unnoticed by Barings for years. He caused over $1 billion of losses and murdered a business pillar of England.

That man is Nick Leeson.

Nick Leeson is exceptionally average looking. He is neither handsome nor ugly with nothing remarkable about his appearance. In fact, if a police sketch artist needed a good starting point from which to draw a middle aged, average caucasian male, Nick's face would be a perfect place to start.

He does not look like the single protagonist of a multi-year fraud that shook the financial world. Of course he does not look like a man who did time in a prison with members of the notorious Triad gang.

But he is both.

In 1992, Nick Leeson became the manager of Barings Bank in Singapore. He seemed an obvious choice because of his stellar record of producing enormous returns for the bank. It seemed the combination of the Asian market and the spectacular track record of Leeson would be recipe for success.

But, Leeson began exceeding the limits of Barings regulations. His unauthorized trades went directly against Barings policies. He was speculating that the Nikkei 225 , Tokyo's version of the DOW Jones Industrial, would make massive gains.

In 1990 the Nikkei had reached heights over 38,000 JPY or Yen. During Lesson's tenure at the Tokyo office of Barings, he watched this particular index slide lower and lower until it was hovering around 20,000 JPY.

In the mind of aggressive traders this was a great opportunity. The index was on sale, and at some point it had to bounce back, or so Leeson thought. So he broke rank, created a fake account numbered 88888 to hide his illegal trades and heavily wagered that the Nikkei would rumble back.

For three years this went on without anyone at Barings auditing Leeson's activity. For three years one man had unchecked access to all of the money managed by one of the oldest banks in existence, and was never audited.

Regretfully during that time the Nikkei slid deeper and deeper into the abyss. Every time it did Barings lost, unchecked money from the 88888 account. So Leeson, like a drunken gambler who lost the rent money, was in a position to cover his losses. And he did it by doubling down on the Nikkei, which would, in turn fall again causing the momentum of the snowball to grow along with it's massive size.

Then Leeson made his biggest mistake. He bought the equivalent of millions of dollars of futures in, what he thought, was a hugely underpriced Japanese market on January 16th, 1995.

But Nick Leeson's timing was horrible.

The very next day, January 17th, 1995, Kobe Japan was torn to pieces by a 7.2 earthquake. What seemed to be an undervalued market was crushed along with billions of dollars of buildings, infrastructure and 6000 people. Twice the amount killed in the US during the attacks on 9/11.

As the world pulled their money out of the Asian market, the Nikkei 225 was reduced from it's former glory at over 38,000 JPY to less than 15,000 JPY that summer. Nick Leeson made a few attempts at a fast recovery, none of which worked out.

When it was all over he left Barings Bank completely broke. His three year tryst lost Barings $1.4 billion and cost over 1000 people their jobs. Many workers, drinking in pubs in

England had more money in their pockets than their bank did, as long as they didn't work for Barings.

Incredibly, when the dust settled Leeson was only sentenced to 6 1/2 years of a possible 80+ year sentence. Of the 6 1/2 years he only served four. Today, the man who crushed Barings is a world famous speaker, author and by most accounts, a success.

The public is still curious how Nick got away with such a short sentence.

The answer has everything to do with the people around Leeson, and their thresholds.

In May of 1978 the American Journal of Sociology published Mark Granovetter's Threshold Models of Collective Behavior. Up to that point conventional wisdom held that people either did or did not participate in activities such as spreading rumors, riots, and protests. Either you were comfortable in socially disagreeable settings or you weren't, the thinking went.

But Granovetter didn't believe that to be true. So he set out to prove that it wasn't. In the study he describes his findings in the context of riots. Who does and does not participate in riots and at what point will a typical non-rioter change their mind and join the riot.

His findings show that people are not binary in their thinking, even though most of us claim to be. We feel like we are or are not the type of person who would join a riot.

But that isn't accurate.

The truth is that most of us are not the type of person to join a riot unless a certain number and type of person is rioting. If the people from our church, and our parents and one of our grandmothers is rioting we may decide to join.

This unknown number of people who have to be rioting for us to join is our riot participation threshold. Some of us have a threshold of 1. All it takes is one person to throw a rock through a window for us to join in. Others may be a 5 and still other are a 30, and need the whole neighborhood to join before they will participate. In the study Granovetter explains it this way.

-Imagine 100 people milling around in a square-a potential riot situation. Suppose their riot threshold are distributed as follows: there is one individual with threshold 0, one with threshold 1, one with threshold 2, and so on up to the last individual with threshold 99. This is a uniform distribution of thresholds. The outcome is clear and could be described as a "bandwagon" or "domino" effect: the person with threshold 0, the "instigator" engages in riot behavior-breaks a window say. This activates the person with threshold 1; the activity of these two people then activates the person with threshold 2, and so on, until all 100 people have joined. The equilibrium is 100.

Now perturb this distribution as follows. Remove the individual with threshold 1 and replaced him by one with threshold 2. By all of our usual ways of describing groups of people, the two crowds are essentially identical. But the outcome in the second case is quite different-the instigator riots, but there is now no one with threshold 1, and so the riot ends at that point, with one rioter.-

Granovetter goes on to explain the reality of threshold distribution. That in a group of 100 there is a mean, or average threshold. As each individual has a threshold, so does the group. If the mean threshold of the group is 25, once 25 people are rioting, the entire group joins in and the riot explodes, sometimes literally.

The riot can go from a small group of disgruntled people, to a national event depending on the thresholds of the people involved.

But if it weren't for the people with low thresholds, the 1's and 2's in the group, nothing would happen. The group may have a mean threshold of 25, but if the first 25 people don't start rioting, the group remains docile.

Every group has a mean threshold before the group acts as a whole, and the dynamic of the group and the situation play a big role as well. Imagine for a moment that same group of rioters is watching a movie in a theater.

Now what is the mean threshold of the group to walk out of the movie?

It all depends. If the group is rioting out of frustration over a white cop shooting an unarmed black student at a local college with no apparent reason, and the movie is about the struggles of growing up as a black youth in a large city, the group probably won't leave the theater at all. They have a very high movie-leaving threshold, at least for that movie.

But if the group is rioting because they are heavily Christian, and the Ten Commandments was taken off of a public building, and the movie has swearing, nudity and R-rated content, the mean threshold of that group to leave the theater, in the very same movie is much lower than the previous group.

Dr. James Fallon, the neuroscientist we discussed earlier, who learned that he was a psychopath, offers a perfect example of group thresholds in his book. Between 1990 and 1991 he was in Kenya, when he witnessed an example of mirror neurons at work. You may remember that we discussed mirror neurons in chapter 9, the chapter involving Milton Erickson and mirroring.

Dr. Fallon explains that he and his brother Tom found themselves in a village led by an elder named Bernard. This was near the Ugandan border where most of the villagers had never seen a white person, let alone played the horrible game of golf.

He and his brother had a set of golf clubs and found a spot in which to practice. This piqued the curiosity of the villagers. After they watched Dr. Fallon and his brother both hit golf balls, Dr. Fallon asked if they would like to learn (as if the white race hasn't brought about enough trauma to the tribes of Africa.)

This is the story as told by Dr. Fallon.

-Among the 100 or so amassed there, a few brave souls stepped forward, including the family elder. A gentleman of about 80 years who was dressed in a full suit and a hat with a Christian cross emblazoned on it. They first watched as I flubbed a shot about 30 yards drawing a chuckle from Bernard and a belly laugh from Tom.

Then Tom stepped forward and blasted a 3 wood to the very end of the field and there were gasps of awe from the gathered clan. Then the elder stepped forward, grabbed one of the clubs, an implement he had never seen, let alone used before, and took a quick and furious swing at the teed up golf ball. He whiffed it, but no one made a peep. Then within 3 seconds, as if clearing a field with a scythe, he swung at the ball again, catching it on the sweet spot, and the ball took off about 150 yards, with a hint of a slice.

Applause erupted from all of us. Then, one-by-one every man, woman and child stepped forward and missed with the first swing and then nailed the ball with the second. Some of the adult men drove the ball more than 200 yards. This was an example of the mirror neuron system cranking away with all cylinders firing. The next year when I visited the village it was like they had created their own two-hole golf association, an effect I had never intended to curse them with in the first place.-

In Dr. Fallon's example, the village had the perfect threshold and influencers for golf to infect the entire village with the epidemic. Apparently the elder had a threshold of either 1 or 2 for the game of golf.

He need only see Dr. Fallon and maybe his brother Tom golfing before he felt comfortable enough to give it a try. Perhaps the next person who tried had a threshold of 1, 2 or 3, or perhaps their threshold was that the elder had to try first before they would.

Dr. Fallon is not clear on whether or not the tribe has sued him for the introduction of a disease more wretched than smallpox.

This is the crux of influence. The dynamic of thresholds and context is the heart of persuasion and influence. In order to affect group behavior, that group needs the mean number of people to make the change first. Those people must have a low threshold and be the proper influencers to instigate the change, or it won't happen. But if that recipe is not just right, the blaze will not catch on.

For instance, why did Justine Sacco's tweet go viral? When she wrote, "Going to Africa. Hope I don't get AIDS. Just kidding. I'm white!" she only had 170 followers, which is nothing in the world of Twitter.

Let's also realize that there are tweets happening daily from people with whom we are familiar, that are just as inflammatory as this one. But they don't go viral and ruin careers.

Here are just a few inflammatory remarks made on Twitter by famous people that didn't ruin careers.

World famous movie critic, Roger Ebert tweeted, "Friends don't let jackasses drink and drive." after the death of Ryan Dunn from the Jackass movie franchise. Ryan died in an alcohol involved car accident with his friend Zachary Hartwell.

Entertainer Kanye West wrote, "An abortion can cost a ballin' nigga up to 10gs maybe a 100. Gold diggin' bitches be getting pregnant on purpose."

Finally, after a highly publicized domestic violence incident in which Rihanna was left battered by her then beau Chris Brown, Amanda Bynes tweeted, "@rihanna, Chris Brown beat you because you're not pretty enough."

Those tweets may have spread and become infamous, but did not garner near the reaction that Justine's did. These are people whose tweets are often read by more people in one second that Justine had on her entire account.

But Justine's tweet found it's way to a man named Sam Biddle. He was the editor of Valleywag which was a leg of Gawker media. When he saw what he decided was a racist tweet from a senior IAC employee, he was at his threshold for sharing and mocking a tweet. He shared it on Valleywag's blog where it exploded and went on to get over 200k responses from an audience with a very low threshold for social shaming.

The opposite happens when a group has a very high threshold for something. In a situation where change needs to happen, if the group is resistant to the change, or lacking the influencers to reach the groups threshold, the culture of, "this is how it's done around here" runs rampant. Unfortunately for the customers of Barings bank, the employees had a very high threshold for pointing out glaring problems

For example, the now famous 5-8's account where Leeson made the illegal trades, showed up every day in the bank's fledgeling IT department. Every day when the odd account number showed up, the IT professional would simply delete it off of his screen, rather than investigate.

Nick explained the culture around the fraud during an interview with Nick Batsford on CORE Finance. He says, "I was never challenged, lots of diaspora, technology not communicating with each other, people not asking sensible questions and any challenges that were made were completely superficial, easily to divert, pretty much me just giving cock and ball answers on the spot as the questions were asked."

He faked it.

He faked it and no one had the appropriate, personal threshold to question what he was doing. And Barings lacked the collective threshold to hold up their own policies.

This is part of why Leeson received such lenient sentence. Yes he perpetrated a fraud that ruined entire lives. Yes he lied, cheated and stole. But he did it in a bank with over 200 years of experience. The people who trusted Barings did so based on the sheer amount of time they had been on the planet. When you have been in business 230 years you should have some regulations in place, which they did.

Unfortunately no one wanted to be disagreeable enough to enforce those regulations.

The IT person didn't take the time to check account number 88888. Leeson's own management let him facilitate this fraud for three years. Much like Bernie Madoff, it may never have come to light if it weren't for outside forces. In Bernies case the 2008 sub-prime lending collapse, in this case an earthquake.

So Leeson gets a portion of the blame, but so does Barings, for allowing a culture with such a high threshold to exist. The Board of Banking Supervision of the Bank of England launched an investigation led by Britain's Chancellor of the Exchequer who released a report on July 18, 1995. Lord Bruce of Donington, in the House of Lords' debate on the report, said:

-Even the provisional conclusions of the report are interesting. I should like to give them to the House so that we may be reminded what the supervisory body itself decided at the end of such investigation as it was able to make. It stated on page 250:

"Barings' collapse was due to the unauthorised and ultimately catastrophic activities of, it appears, one individual (Leeson) that went undetected as a consequence of a failure of management and other internal controls of the most basic kind".

The words I venture to emphasise to your Lordships are these:

"as a consequence of a failure of management and other internal controls of the most basic kind".

Noble Lords who have read through paragraph 14.2 of the report will be aware that it specifies these deficiencies. The report states:

"Management teams have a duty to understand fully the businesses they manage."

Really! They really have to understand the businesses! I would have thought that it was an elementary assumption to make that the controllers should understand the nature of the businesses they are trying to control. The next requirement is this:

"Responsibility for each business activity has to be clearly established and communicated".

Hooray for that! I wonder how businesses in this country manage in their generality to continue without that qualification. The third requirement is:

"Clear segregation of duties is fundamental to any effective control system."

Tut, tut! We are now treating the real elementum of the whole art and science of management, and it needs to be repeated here. The report continues:

"Relevant internal controls, including independent risk management, have to be established for all business activities."

Hooray for that! These are matters of plain, ordinary common sense. One does not need to be an accountant or a management consultant to be aware of that. Finally:

"Top management and the Audit Committee have to ensure that significant weaknesses, identified to them by internal audit or otherwise, are resolved quickly."

Well, well, well! These are all respects which this control body finds were absent from Barings. Do noble Lords really know what is being said? It is being said that Barings ought not to have been authorised bankers from the beginning, because any business — I do not care whether it is a whelk stall (one must not insult whelk stall owners in the context of this catastrophe) or what — knows that these are the basic conditions for the continuance of the business. It seems to me that the Bank of England ought never to have authorised this concern without verifying that all these conditions were in place.-

In other words, Barings threshold for managing their own business was way out of whack.

And so is ours.

Barings gets some of the blame for allowing this corruption to exist. And we should get some of the blame for the manner in which we view, and treat those with autism.

The final trait of people on the spectrum that we are exploring is that they open new doors for neurotypicals. But if we plan to walk through the new doors open by them, we have to lower certain thresholds, which is exactly what the next, and final chapter explains.

The Beginning

Chapter 13
influence achieved?

Progress is impossible without change, and those who cannot change their minds cannot change anything. -George Bernard Shaw

The next few sentences should break your heart.

In a study on children with autism in social settings, Erin Rotheram-Fuller, Connie Kasari and Jill Locke demonstrated what it is like growing up on the spectrum today and what changes need to take place. The trio measured friendship quality in groups involving children with autism. They found, among other things, that children with autism attempt to initiate friendships to the same degree as neurotypical children.

In other words they want to have friends just like any other kids.

But the hurtful part of the story is those attempts are reciprocated 50% less if they came from someone on the spectrum, than if they came from a neurotypical child. It is twice as hard for a kid with autism to make friends as a kid without it.

If the image of a kid with ASD being shunned at school doesn't break your heart, I can't help you.

The threshold for students in our society to accept those on the spectrum is very, very high. In fact the study blatantly explains it this way:

-A large body of literature has examined the peer relationships of children with ASD and has shown some specific social difficulties children with ASD face in school.

In particular, researchers have found that children with ASD have fewer friendships, report more loneliness and poorer friendship quality, and are less socially included and accepted into their classroom's social structure as compared to their typically developing classmates.-

The phrase "pena ajena" is Spanish. It doesn't exactly translate into English, but it loosely means to feel shame for someone else. When a child with ASD is admitted to school, the entire system feels pena ajena for them.

The other students may wave and make them the equivalent of a mascot, but they aren't becoming friends. The administration may smile while they stick them in a class for "special" people and sweep them under the rug for a dozen years. This feeling of shame is not lost on those people. They feel it in the form of the loneliness mentioned above.

But our pena ajena for those with autism is not only hurting them, it is hurting us as well.

Some of the greatest contributions to society have come from people on the spectrum. We have already discussed people like Isaac Newton and Alan Turing, but it is widely accepted that Nicola Tesla, Hans Christian Andersen, Lewis Carroll and Mozart were also on the spectrum. Temple Grandin, who is verifiably on the spectrum, revolutionized the cattle industry.

Adam Smith wrote The Theory of Moral Sentiments and The Wealth of Nations, which is the pivotal cornerstone and foundation of ethical capitalism. Fundamentally it teaches that capitalism can be good if it is used the right way, if workers are treated well and if the wealthy are held to certain standards. This brilliant work is still light years ahead of the system we use today.

Adam Smith is often considered to have been on the spectrum. His personality and social quirks are captured in the book, The Man Who Found Time: James Hutton and the Discovery of the Earth's Antiquity. The following is an excerpt.

-He [Adam Smith] cut quite a figure. He always carried a cane, but never used it—rather he rested it on his shoulder "as a soldier carries his musket." He dressed well, but not extravagantly. Like Hutton, he struck observers with his eccentricities because he often talked to himself, and his head turned from side to side while he walked. One of his biographers commented, "Often, moreover, his lips would be moving all the while, and smiling in rapt conversation with invisible companions.-

But this brilliant man did not do his work in an obscure corner of a home only to be discovered later by someone with the social wherewithal to decipher it. Adam Smith worked together with his close friend, Benjamin Franklin developing the work. In March of 1924, the Academy of Political Science published an article named The Relations Between Adam Smith and Benjamin Franklin Before 1776. The first paragraph says this.

-It was claimed by the late Dr. Simon N. Patten that The Wealth of Nations is a defense of the colonies, and an attack on the English colonial system. It was claimed that, but for Benjamin Franklin, Adam Smith would have written the treatise on politics promised in the passage at the end of The Theory of Moral Sentiments. Franklin was sent to England twice on missions to Parliament, as representatives of agent of Pennsylvania, and by appointment, of other colonies; from 1757 to 1762, and again from December, 1764, to 1775, inclusive. It was said that he went to Scotland to see Smith, with a view of persuading him to write a treatise on colonial policy; or, at least, that when they met, Franklin urged such a task upon him. They were said to have been close friends, and in frequent communication with each other.-

"They were said to hav been close friends, and in frequent communications with each other." Not only did the Scottish man with ASD not struggle making friends, but Benjamin Franklin sailed across the Atlantic to reach out and connect with him. This is a far cry from what those with autism face today on the playground. It seems that our threshold for accepting people on the spectrum is much higher than it was in the 1700's.

So our acceptance of those with ASD has shrunk, but autism diagnoses have exploded. 1 in 68 people are diagnosed with the disorder today. That is up 30 percent from the 1 in 88 rate reported in 2008, and more than double the 1 in 150 rate in 2000. In fact, the diagnoses has trended steeply upward since the early 1990s, in the U.S. and globally.

These numbers come from Maureen Durkin, who is the chair of the Department of Population Health Sciences and the Evan and Marion Helfaer Professor of Public Health at the University of Wisconsin School of Medicine and Public Health.

We are obsessed with claiming that people have ASD, but once we label them, our threshold for accepting them is abysmal. This means we have decided to shun one of the largest growing portions of our demographic. Not to mention they are the portion responsible for some of the most amazing contributions to society.

All moral and ethical reasons aside, this trend is dangerous. For completely selfish reasons alone we should realize that we are isolating one of the most productive and contributory segments of the population. But when you add moral relevance and dignity to the mix, this high threshold for accepting autism is ridiculous and must change.

But big changes can be great.

When a forest fire rips through an overgrown forest, the wake is devastating. Living in Arizona, I have witnessed, first-hand the destruction of some of the largest and most destructive forest fires in history. The Wallow Fire destroyed over 538,000 acres of land in which I grew up. It was stopped within sight of my childhood home where my parents still live today. In some areas of the pine forest near my hometown the pristine wilderness could only be described as "moonscaped" because it looked to us like the surface of the moon, after the fire obliterated it. But then a funny thing happened.

In the years since that fire some of the wildlife populations have exploded, new saplings are growing where no light could possibly reach through the thick canopy before. Tall ground cover has given refugee for baby elk, deer and antelope to hide from predators, and we have learned better ways of managing the forest than the basic abandonment that occurred in the decades prior to the fire. This is the Intermediate Disturbance Hypothesis at work.

The IDH says that an ecosystem flourishes when a disturbance occurs, occasionally. That when you turn a rock over from the position it's held for 15 years, the change may kill some of the life on top and underneath the rock, but in the long run it's healthy. In the long run the new exposure of sunlight causes new growth, the rich material from the ground that is now on the top of the rock feeds animals that didn't have access to it before and the earth where the rock used to lay is rich with fertilizer to grow new life.

When a disturbance happens with the right frequency it is good for the environment, and we are due for a disturbance.

It is time that we take a long hard look at the society we have built that excludes some of the most influential and contributory of our population. The struggles many people on the spectrum have is completely social. We don't think they smile when they should, they may not laugh at our jokes or they may say exactly what is on their mind. These are not problems to society, they are issues with social norms, and social norms change all the time.

From hair cuts to the way our pants fit to the style of cars we drive, we are forever in the ebb and flow of shifting social norms. Our level of acceptance and integration of people with mild ASD is nothing more than an opinion. It's an opinion that, in many cases, needs to change collectively. But, as we discussed in the last chapter, the threshold we have for this change is higher than the amount of people acting on the change.

We cannot change the collective threshold of our society, only the number of people working to reach that threshold. Since taking on this project I have had the opportunity to speak with business owners and leaders all over the U.S. about this topic. Inevitably the question comes up when they ask, "If people on the spectrum are so influential, should my next sales person have ASD?"

This speaks to the heart of the problem.

I have a canned answer which I offer to this question that, I think gets us closer to reaching the ASD acceptance threshold. I say, " Your next sales person should be passionate, rarely judge others, play fewer head games, not be tied to social expectations, live in the moment and open new doors for neurotypicals. If you find that person, it shouldn't matter if someone has deemed them an aspie, on the spectrum, as having ASD or a weirdo. If they meet your criteria, hire them."

We have become obsessed with labeling people. The DSM is the Diagnostic and Statistical Manual of Mental Disorders and is the bible of labeling people. The DSM started at 130 pages and 106 mental disorders in 1952. Then it went to 492 pages and 265 disorders in 1980. The new DSM-5 is 947 pages long and lists thing like caffeine withdrawal as a disorder.

They have labeled shy people with avoidant personality disorder and were responsible for segmenting autism into two disorders-Autism and Aspergers. In fact slate.com ran the numbers and realized that over half of the US population will qualify as having a disorder. We are more likely to have a disorder than to not have one!

When over half a population is affected by something it is no longer a disorder.

It is order.

We are designed to be different. The order of life **is** disorder. At what point do we stop trying to define "normal" in a human population that has never, ever been similar to each other? Every time a population tries to make one segment normal and the rest abnormal we have problems.

For centuries normal meant believing that everything was made of earth, wind, fire and water, not of atomos. Those who were abnormal were heretics. Democritus had his books burned for his abnormality, and Socrates was executed for it.

For a time the world tried to make men normal while women and children weren't valued at all. In some cases they were property because they didn't fit the right mold. King Leupold II cut off their hands and feet to motivate his workers.

In the US for a time being white was normal and all other races weren't. It took a decades-long civil rights movement to begin making changes to that thinking.

When we try to create a norm it forces us to label everyone who isn't that thing. They are transgender, redneck, ADHD, progressive, hunters, non-union, ethnic or a million other adjectives.

Yet the man whose adjective labeled him accurately as one of the most terrible men on the planet, saw something in this "disorder" that we don't. Ivan the Terrible saw someone whose point of view was valuable. A man with almost no regard for human life, had regard for what he saw in Basil.

How far fetched is it to think that an ancient society knew something we don't?

In June of 1992 in Longyou County, China, a villager discovered something we can't explain today. While pumping water from a local, "bottomless" lake he found hand carved caverns filled with decorative wall art, man made support columns and the most amazing pattern of what appear to be chisel marks on the wall, floors and ceiling of the cave. Scientists have dated the caves back to before 200 B.C.

This is before the time we think anyone had the technology to build this type of cave. The perfectly uniform chisel marks on the walls of the cave match machine digging better than hand carving. What's more, there is no written record of the construction of the Longyou Caves, despite the people of the time being fabulous record keepers. This is a structure we can't understand.

Not unlike the wall at Sacsayhuaman.

In the southern part of Peru is the town of Sacsayhuaman. This is the home of an engineering feat that seems more difficult to explain than the building of the Great Pyramids in Egypt. The wall is made of solid stones weighing up to 20 tons and by most accounts was built 1000 years ago.

Just deciphering how people, who we assume didn't have the capability to cut or moved these stones is difficult. But add that none of the stones is a uniform shape and each stone is cut perfectly to fit the stones around it and it is a feat of engineering that we can't replicate today.

There are stones cut to make the shape of flowers locked in place by the stones around it, many feet thick. The stones fit together so well that no mortar was used in the joints of the wall and it has withstood an unknown number of earthquakes without falling.

From Mayan calendars to Roman dodecahedrons, it is clear that there were ancient societies who knew things we do not. And yet we feel we are the most advanced. We feel that we understand life and humans enough to classify the problems and malfunctions in over 50% of the population whom we have decided don't fit in. Today it takes a book like the DSM-5, which is almost 1000 pages to classify and label those people.

But when those labels reach over 50% of the population, maybe it's time to face the fact that none of us are normal.

We all have a disorder compared to someone else. But we all have a gift as well. Maybe it takes a different type of person than us to come up with different ideas. Ideas like computers, physics, ethical capitalism and those we have yet to consider don't come from average minds.

Influential ideas come from influential people and history has proven those with ASD extremely influential.

We owe it to ourselves, but more importantly to them, to treat them well and understand them for who they really are.

They are the gift of a different, often better, perspective.

Unless someone like you cares a whole awful lot,
nothing is going to get better
... It's not.

-Dr. Seuss

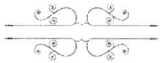

Made in the USA
Middletown, DE
13 September 2018